The God Who Loves

The God Who Loves

by

John MacArthur, Jr.

W PUBLISHING GROUP™

www.wpublishinggroup.com

A Division of Thomas Nelson, Inc.
www.ThomasNelson.com

ISBN 978-1-4002-7794-0

04 05 06 07   9 8 7 6

Printed in the United States of America

To Patricia,

whom I love more than life itself
and whose love for me
is closer to heavenly perfection
than anything I have known on earth.

Contents

Contents

Introduction

A FEW YEARS AGO I had the opportunity to spend several days traveling with Bill and Gloria Gaither, the well-known gospel musicians. At one point I asked Bill what, in his estimation, were the greatest Christian lyrics ever written—aside from the inspired Psalms.

Without hesitation, he began quoting the words from F. M. Lehman's "The Love of God:"

> The love of God is greater far
> Than tongue or pen can ever tell;
> It goes beyond the highest star,
> And reaches to the lowest hell.
> The guilty pair, bowed down with care,
> God gave His Son to win;
> His erring child He reconciled,
> And pardoned from his sin.
>
> When hoary time shall pass away,
> And earthly thrones and kingdoms fall,
> When men who here refuse to pray,

The God Who Loves

On rocks and hills and mountains call,
God's love so sure, shall still endure,
All measureless and strong;
Redeeming grace to Adam's race—
The saints' and angels' song.

Could we with ink the ocean fill,
And were the skies of parchment made,
Were every stalk on earth a quill,
And every man a scribe by trade,
To write the love of God above
Would drain the ocean dry.
Nor could the scroll contain the whole,
Though stretched from sky to sky.

O love of God, how rich and pure!
How measureless and strong!
It shall forevermore endure—
The saints' and angels' song.

No lyrics in all hymnody surpass the third stanza of that song, he said.

Indeed, few rivals come to mind. The poetry alone is beautiful—but the meaning is profound.

As I pondered that song, my mind was flooded with echoes from Scripture. "God is love," the apostle John wrote (1 Jn. 4:8, 16). "His lovingkindness is everlasting" is the refrain for all twenty-six verses of Psalm 136. Those same words appear at least forty-one times in the Old Testament. God's lovingkindness is better than life itself, the psalmist reminds us (Ps. 63:3). God is "merciful and gracious, slow to anger and abundant in lovingkindness and truth (Ps. 86:15)." He "is good; His lovingkindness is everlasting" (Ps. 100:5).

Elsewhere the psalmist writes, "How precious is Thy lovingkindness, O God! And the children of men take refuge in the shadow of Thy wings" (Ps. 36:7). And "I will sing of the loving-kindess of the Lord forever. . . . Lovingkindness will be built up forever" (Ps. 89:1–2).

The New Testament unveils the ultimate proof of God's love: "But God demonstrates His own love toward us, in that while we were yet sinners, Christ died for us" (Rom. 5:8). "By this the love of God was manifested in us, that God has sent His only begotten Son into the world so that we might live through Him. In this is love, not that we loved God, but that He loved us and sent His Son to be the propitiation for our sins" (1 Jn. 4:9–10). "God, being rich in mercy, because of His great love with which He loved us . . . made us alive together with Christ (by grace you have been saved), and raised us up with Him, and seated us with Him in the heavenly places, in Christ Jesus" (Eph. 2:4–6).

And the most familiar verse of all says this: "For God so loved the world, that He gave His only begotten Son, that whoever believes in Him should not perish, but have eternal life" (Jn. 3:16).

No wonder the apostle exults, "See how great a love the Father has bestowed upon us. . . ." (1 Jn. 3:1).

Obviously, God's love and goodness are persistent themes in both the Old and New Testaments. If the amount of space the Bible gives the subject is any indication, hardly any truth about God is as important as His love. On almost every page of Scripture we see divine goodness, tender mercies, lovingkind-ness, patience, longsuffering, and grace. All those virtues are expressions of God's love.

The doctrine of God's love is by no means simple. It raises a host of philosophical and theological difficulties. For example, some of the most obvious questions it brings up are these: If God is so loving, why does He send people to hell? Why does He allow sin and suffering and pain and sorrow? How can holocausts and natural disasters and other forms of mass destruction and human suffering exist in a universe designed by a God who is truly loving? Why did God allow the human race to be plunged into sin in the first place?

In all honesty we need to acknowledge the difficulty of questions like those. All of us have asked them. Many of us have been challenged with such questions from skeptics who ask us to provide satisfactory answers. If we're honest, we must admit that the answers are not easy. God Himself has not seen fit to reveal full answers to some of those questions. Instead, He reveals Himself as loving, all-wise, perfectly righteous, and supremely good—and He simply bids us trust Him.

That becomes easier the better we understand what Scripture teaches about the love of God. In this book we will grapple with some of those difficult questions about God's love, but not until we've laid a good foundation for understanding what Scripture means when it says, "God is love."

We must also note that several of the very worst corruptions of Christian truth are based on the notion that God can be understood solely in terms of His love. Those who hold such a perspective often refuse to acknowledge God's wrath against sin, because they believe He cannot be *both* loving *and* angry with sinners. Others, perhaps intending to dissociate God from the tragedies and terrors of human experience, reason that if God is truly loving, He can't possibly be all-powerful; otherwise, He would put a stop to all suffering.

On the other hand, some well-meaning Christians concerned with doctrinal orthodoxy are so cautious about overemphasizing God's love that they fear to speak of it at all. Our culture, after all, is "in love" with sin and self-love, and utterly dull to the wrath of God against sin. Isn't it counterproductive to preach the love of God in the midst of such an ungodly society? Some who reason thus tend to see every bad thing that happens as if it were a direct judgment from the hand of a severe Deity.

Both extremes paint a distorted picture of God and further confuse the issue of understanding God's love.

As long as we stay within the bounds of biblical truth about God's love, we can avoid both of these transgressions. As we examine what the Bible says about this subject, we will see how wonderfully God's love can be presented to sinners and how perfectly it fits with His hatred of sin. And the things hard to understand are made easier.

In our pursuit of understanding on this matter, however, we must be willing to shed a lot of popular, sentimental notions about divine love. Many of our favorite presuppositions about God need to be corrected. God's love and His holiness must be carefully understood in light of His wrath against sin. We must see love from the divine perspective before we can truly grasp the import of God's great love for us.

The remedy, as always, is an open-hearted embracing of all the biblical data. And it is my design in this book to try to highlight a broad, balanced cross-section of that data. As the songwriter pointed out, to cover the subject as it deserves to be covered would drain the oceans of ink and fill a galaxy of skies. And even after many eons, the preface would barely be written.

Eternity will be spent in just such a study, I am sure. That's why for me, the opportunity to write this book has been like a little slice of heaven. As you read, I hope you will sense something of the heavenly glory as well, and learn that all the sadness, pain, and sorrow of human life do not negate the love of God to humanity. On the contrary; it is only the knowledge of His love in the midst of such trials that enables us to endure and be strengthened by them.

We'll spend the first three chapters laying a foundation for understanding God's love. Beginning in chapter 4, we will return to deal with the hard questions we raised here, such as why God allows suffering. In the chapters that follow, we'll see how God's love defines who He is, how it applies to all humanity, and how it applies in a unique and special way to Christians.

My prayer for all who read this book is an echo of Paul's prayer for the Ephesians:

". . . that Christ may dwell in your hearts through faith; and that you, being rooted and grounded in love, may be able to comprehend with all the saints what is the breadth, and height and depth, and to know the love of Christ which surpasses knowledge, that you may be filled up to all the fulness of God" (Eph. 3:17–19).

God So Loved the World

God's Love in Recent Church History

God's Love and the Contemporary Church

God's Love for the Unbelieving World

Chapter 1

God So Loved the World

Love is the best known but least understood of all God's attributes. Almost everyone who believes in God these days believes that He is a God of love. I have even met agnostics who are quite certain that *if* God exists, He must be benevolent, compassionate, and loving.

All those things *are* infinitely true about God, of course, but not the way most people think. Because of the influence of modern liberal theology, many suppose that God's love and goodness ultimately nullify His righteousness, justice, and holy wrath. They envision God as a benign heavenly grandfather—tolerant, affable, lenient, permissive, devoid of any real displeasure over sin, who without consideration of His holiness will benignly pass over sin and accept people as they are.

God's Love in Recent Church History

People in past generations often went to the opposite extreme. They tended to think of God as stern, demanding, cruel, even abusive. They so magnified God's wrath that they virtually

1

ignored His love. Little more than a hundred years ago, nearly all evangelistic preaching portrayed God only as a fierce Judge whose fury burned against sinners. History reveals that some dramatic shifts in how we think of God have taken place over the past three centuries.

Jonathan Edwards

PERHAPS THE MOST FAMOUS sermon ever preached in America was Jonathan Edwards's "Sinners in the Hands of an Angry God." Edwards was a pastor in colonial Massachusetts and a brilliant theological mind. He preached his most famous sermon as a guest speaker in a church at Enfield, Connecticut, on July 8, 1741. This sermon sparked one of the most dramatic episodes of revival in the Great Awakening. Here is an excerpt that shows the preacher's graphic and frightening bluntness in portraying God's dreadful wrath against sinners:

> The God that holds you over the pit of hell, much as one holds a spider, or some loathsome insect over the fire, abhors you, and is dreadfully provoked: his wrath towards you burns like fire; he looks upon you as worthy of nothing else, but to be cast into the fire; he is of purer eyes than to bear to have you in his sight; you are ten thousand times more abominable in his eyes, than the most hateful venomous serpent is in ours. You have offended him infinitely more than ever a stubborn rebel did his prince; and yet it is nothing but his hand that holds you from falling into the fire every moment. It is to be ascribed to nothing else, that you did not go to hell the last night; that you was suffered to awake again in this world, after you closed your eyes to sleep. And there is no other reason to be given, why you have not dropped into hell since you arose in the morning, but that God's hand has held you up. There is no other reason to be

given why you have not gone to hell, since you have sat here in the house of God, provoking his pure eyes by your sinful wicked manner of attending his solemn worship. Yea, there is nothing else that is to be given as a reason why you do not this very moment drop down into hell.

O sinner! Consider the fearful danger you are in: it is a great furnace of wrath, a wide and bottomless pit, full of the fire of wrath, that you are held over in the hand of that God, whose wrath is provoked and incensed as much against you, as against many of the damned in hell. You hang by a slender thread, with the flames of divine wrath flashing about it, and ready every moment to singe it, and burn it asunder; and you have no interest in any Mediator, and nothing to lay hold of to save yourself, nothing to keep off the flames of wrath, nothing of your own, nothing that you ever have done, nothing that you can do, to induce God to spare you one moment.

The language and imagery were so vivid that many people who heard Edwards trembled, some cried out for mercy, and others fainted.

Our generation—weaned on "Jesus loves me! this I know"—finds Edwards's famous sermon shocking for an altogether different reason. Most people today would be appalled that anyone would describe God in such terrifying terms.

But it is important that we understand the context of Edwards's sermon. Edwards was no fiery emotionalist; he appealed dispassionately to his hearers' sense of reason—even reading his message in a carefully controlled tone lest anyone be emotionally manipulated. His message ended with a tender appeal to flee to Christ for mercy. One observer who was present that evening recorded that "Several Souls were hopefully wrought upon [that] night, & oh ye cheerfulness and pleasantness of their countenances [that] receivd comfort—oh [that] God wd strengthen and confirm—we sung an hymn & prayd & dismissd ye Assembly."[1] So the overall tenor of that evening's service was decidedly uplifting. It signaled a time of great revival throughout New England.

Edwards has been falsely caricatured by some as a harsh and pitiless preacher who took great delight in frightening his congregations with colorful descriptions of the torments of hell. Nothing could be further from the truth. He was a warm and sensitive pastor as well as a meticulous theologian, and he stood on solid biblical ground when he characterized God as an angry Judge. Scripture tells us, "God judgeth the righteous, and God is angry with the wicked every day" (Ps. 7:11, KJV). Edwards's sermon that night was an exposition of Deuteronomy 32:35–36: "To me belongeth vengeance, and recompense; their foot shall slide in due time: for the day of their calamity is at hand, and the things that shall come upon them make haste. For the Lord shall judge his people" (KJV). Those are biblical truths that do need to be proclaimed. And when Jonathan Edwards preached them, he did so with a humble heart of loving compassion. A broader look at his ministry reveals that he also heavily emphasized the grace and love of God. This sermon alone does not give us the full picture of what his preaching was like.

Yet Edwards was not reluctant to preach the unvarnished truth of divine wrath. He saw conversion as the loving work of God in the human soul, and he knew the truth of Scripture was the means God uses to convert sinners. He believed his responsibility as a preacher was to declare both the positive and the negative aspects of that truth as plainly as possible.

Charles Finney

UNFORTUNATELY, A LATER GENERATION of preachers were not so balanced and careful in their approach to evangelism, and not so sound in their theology. Charles Finney, an early nineteenth-century lawyer-turned-revivalist, saw conversion as a *human* work. Finney declared that revival could virtually be manufactured if preachers would employ the right means. He wrote:

> There is nothing in religion beyond the ordinary powers of nature. It consists entirely in the *right exercise* of the powers of nature. It is just that, and nothing else. . . . A revival is not a miracle, nor dependent on a miracle, in any sense. It is a purely philosophical result of the right use of the constituted means—as much so as any other effect produced by the application of means.[2]

Finney even denied that the new birth is a sovereign work of the Holy Spirit (cf. Jn. 3:8). He taught instead that regeneration is something accomplished by the sinner: "The Spirit of God, by the truth, *influences* the sinner to change, and in this sense is the efficient Cause of the change. *But the sinner actually changes, and is therefore himself, in the most proper sense, the author of the change. . . .* A change of heart is *the sinner's own act*."[3]

Finney believed that people could be psychologically manipulated into responding to the gospel. One of his favorite measures for heightening emotions was preaching passionately about the fiery threats of divine vengeance. By this he sought to intimidate people into responding to the gospel. Whereas Edwards had looked to the Holy Spirit to use the truth of Scripture to convert sinners, Finney believed it was the preacher's task to evoke the desirable response, through artful persuasion, browbeating, manipulation, or whatever means possible. He found that terrorizing people was a very effective method of arousing a response. His repertoire was filled with sermons designed to heighten the fears of unbelievers.

Preachers who adopted Finney's methods often carried them to preposterous extremes. Preaching about divine wrath was often merely theatrical. And the subject of God's wrath against sin began to be preached to the exclusion of God's love.

5

The God Who Loves

D. L. Moody

ALL THIS HAD A VERY PROFOUND IMPACT on the popular perception of God. The typical Christian of the mid-1800s would have been scandalized by the suggestion that God loves sinners. Even D. L. Moody, so well-known for his strong emphasis on God's love, wasn't always that way. In fact, he was disturbed the first time he heard another evangelist proclaim God's love for sinners.

The evangelist Moody heard was an unassuming British preacher, converted pickpocket Harry Moorhouse. In the winter of 1868 Moorhouse showed up unexpectedly in Chicago and offered to preach to Moody's congregation. Moody, just leaving for a few days' ministry in St. Louis, was uncertain about Moorhouse's preaching ability. But he had once met Moorhouse while in England, so he reluctantly arranged for the Englishman to speak to a midweek gathering in the church basement.

Returning on Saturday from his trip, Moody asked his wife about Moorhouse's preaching.

"He preaches a little different from you," she told Moody. "He preaches that God loves sinners."

"He is wrong," Moody replied.

Mrs. Moody advised her husband to withhold judgment until she had heard Moorhouse preach. "I think you will agree with him when you hear him, because he backs up everything he says with the Bible."

J. C. Pollock recounts what happened in the few days that followed:

> On Sunday morning Moody noticed his congregation were all carrying Bibles. He had never told them that persons in pews should bring Bibles. "It was something strange to see the people coming in with Bibles, and listen to the flutter of the leaves."
>
> Moorhouse announced his text: "John 3:16: God so loved the world that he gave his only begotten son, that

whosoever believeth in him should not perish but have
everlasting life." Instead of dividing the text into firstly, secondly, thirdly in ministerial manner Moorhouse, Moody
noted, "went from Genesis to Revelation giving proof that
God loves the sinner, and before he got through, two or
three of my sermons were spoiled. . . . I never knew up to
that time that God loved us so much. This heart of mine
began to thaw out; I could not keep back the tears."
Fleming Revell remembered all his long life the sight of
Moody drinking it in on that Sunday morning, February
8th, 1868, and how "on Sunday night little Harry
Moorhouse stood swaying from one foot to another in his
seeming awkwardness, but you forgot all about it as you
heard the message coming from his lips." The text was the
same, "God so loved the world . . ." unfolded once again
from Genesis to Revelation, by a different route, his address
not a sermon so much as a string of related texts or passages, briefly commented upon to form what came to be
known, rather oddly, as a "Bible Reading."

At the end Moody jumped up. "Mr. Moorhouse will
speak every night this week. Everybody come. Tell your
friends to come."

Night after night Moorhouse announced, "God so
loved the world . . ." and drew his hearers by a fresh line
through the Bible: "My friends, for a whole week I have been
trying to tell you how much God loves you, but I cannot do
it with this poor stammering tongue. . . . "

Outside, in the sharp February air, Chicago life rolled on
unawares. Merchants dined and wined, the poor huddled
half-frozen round smoking stoves, sailors from iced-up ships
lechered or boozed or brawled. At Illinois Street among that
crowd of humble citizens and a few new immigrants and a
sprinkle of the rich, the spirit of love ran unfettered. And
D. L. Moody turned in his ways, to become from that time
forth an apostle of the love of God.[4]

That event transformed D. L. Moody's evangelistic style. Moody was subsequently used by God to reach both Britain and America with the simple gospel of love and grace. To people almost utterly unaware of God's lovingkindness, he preached that God is a God of mercy and grace. To multitudes who had been conditioned to think of God only as a wrathful judge, he preached that God is "compassionate and gracious, slow to anger, and abounding in lovingkindness and truth" (Exod. 34:6; cf. 2 Chr. 30:9; Neh. 9:17, 31; Ps. 103:8; 111:4; 112:4; 116:5; Joel 2:13; Jonah 4:2). Moody was instrumental in recovering the truth of divine love from near obscurity.

Modern Liberalism

BUT WITH THE RISE OF LIBERAL THEOLOGY the pendulum swung too far. *Liberalism* (sometimes called *modernism*) was a corruption of Christianity, based on a wholesale denial of the authority and inspiration of Scripture. It was a growing trend throughout the nineteenth century, influenced strongly by trends in German theology. (Friedrich Schliermacher and Albrecht Ritschl were among the leading German theologians responsible for liberalism.) While retaining some of the moral teachings of Christianity, liberalism attacked the historic foundations of the faith. Liberals denied the deity of Christ, the historicity of the Bible, and the uniqueness of the Christian faith. Instead, they proclaimed the brotherhood of all humanity under the fatherhood of God— and consequently insisted that God's only attitude toward humanity was pure love.[5] In fact, the overarching interpretive principle for liberals became the theme of love. If a passage didn't reflect their definition of divine love, it was disallowed as Scripture.[6]

In the early part of this century liberalism took mainline Protestant churches by storm. It might be argued that the first half of the present century ushered in the most serious spiritual decline since the Protestant Reformation. Evangelicalism, which had dominated Protestant America since the days of the founding fathers, was virtually driven out of denominational schools and churches. Evangelicalism managed to survive and even thrive outside the denominations. But it never regained its influence in the mainline groups. Instead it has flourished chiefly in relatively small denominations and non-denominational churches. In a few decades, liberalism virtually destroyed the largest Protestant denominations in America and Europe.

Harry Emerson Fosdick

ONE OF THE MOST POPULAR SPOKESMEN for liberal Christianity was Harry Emerson Fosdick, pastor of the Riverside Church in New York City. Fosdick, while remaining strongly committed to liberal theology, nevertheless acknowledged that the new theology was undermining the concept of a holy God. Contrasting his age with that of Jonathan Edwards, Fosdick wrote:

> Jonathan Edwards' Enfield sermon pictured sinners held over the blazing abyss of hell in the hands of a wrathful deity who at any moment was likely to let go, and so terrific was that discourse in its delivery that women fainted and strong men clung in agony to the pillars of the church. *Obviously, we do not believe in that kind of God any more*, and as always in reaction we swing to the opposite extreme, so in the theology of these recent years we have taught a very mild, benignant sort of deity. . . . Indeed, the god of the new theology has not seemed to care acutely about sin; certainly he has not been warranted to punish heavily; he has been an indulgent parent and when we have sinned, a polite "Excuse me" has seemed more than adequate to make amends.[7]

Fosdick never spoke more truly. He correctly saw that liberalism had led to a warped and imbalanced concept of God. He could even see far enough ahead to realize that liberalism was taking society into a dangerous wasteland of amorality, where "man's sin, his greed, his selfishness, his rapacity roll up across the years an accumulating mass of consequence until at last in a mad collapse the whole earth crashes into ruin."[8]

Despite all that, Fosdick ultimately would not acknowledge the literal reality of God's wrath toward impenitent sinners. To him, "the wrath of God" was nothing more than a metaphor for the natural consequences of wrongdoing. Writing in the wake of World War I, Fosdick suggested that *the moral order of the world has been dipping us in hell.*[9] His theology would not tolerate a personal God whose righteous anger burned against sin. Moreover, to Fosdick, the threat of actual hellfire was only a relic of a barbaric age. *"Obviously, we do not believe in that kind of God any more."*

God's Love and the Contemporary Church

FOSDICK WROTE THOSE WORDS almost eighty years ago. Sadly, what was true of liberalism then is all too true of evangelicalism today. We have lost the reality of God's wrath. We have disregarded His hatred for sin. The God most evangelicals now describe is all-loving and not at all angry. We have forgotten that "It is a terrifying thing to fall into the hands of the living God" (Heb. 10:31). *We do not believe in that kind of God anymore.*

Ironically, this overemphasis on divine beneficence actually works against a sound understanding of God's love. Some theologians are so bent on this perception of God as all love, that when things go wrong they see it as evidence that God can't really control everything. They believe if God is truly loving, He can't be fully sovereign. This view makes God into a victim of evil.[10]

Multitudes have embraced the disastrous idea that God is impotent to deal with evil. They believe He is kindly but feeble, or perhaps aloof, or simply unconcerned about human wickedness. Is it any wonder that people with such a concept of God defy His holiness, take His love for granted, and presume on His grace and mercy? Certainly no one would *fear* a deity like that.

Yet Scripture tells us repeatedly that *fear* of God is the very foundation of true wisdom (Job 28:28; Ps. 111:10; Prov. 1:7; 9:10; 15:33; Mic. 6:9). People often try to explain the sense of those verses away by saying that the "fear" called for is a devout sense of awe and reverence. Certainly the fear of God includes awe and reverence, but it does not *exclude* literal holy terror. "It is the Lord of hosts whom you should regard as holy. And He shall be your fear, and He shall be your dread" (Isa. 8:13).

We must recapture some of the holy terror that comes with a right understanding of God's righteous anger. We need to remember that God's wrath *does* burn against impenitent sinners (Ps. 38:1–3). That reality is the very thing that makes His love so amazing. We must therefore proclaim these truths with the same sense of conviction and fervency we employ when we declare the love of God. It is only against the backdrop of divine wrath that the full significance of God's love can be truly understood. That is precisely the message of the cross of Jesus Christ. After all, it was on the cross that God's love and His wrath converged in all their majestic fullness.

Only those who see themselves as sinners in the hands of an angry God can fully appreciate the magnitude and wonder of His love. In this regard our generation is surely at a greater disadvantage than any previous age. We have been force-fed the doctrines of self-esteem for so long that most people don't really view themselves as sinners worthy of divine wrath. On top of that, religious liberalism, humanism, evangelical compromise, and ignorance of the Scriptures have all worked against a right understanding of who God is. Ironically, in an age that conceives of God as wholly loving, altogether devoid of wrath, few people really understand what God's love is all about!

The God Who Loves

How we address the misconception of the present age is crucial. We must not respond to an overemphasis on divine love by denying that God is love. Our generation's imbalanced view of God cannot be corrected by an equal imbalance in the opposite direction. I am frankly fearful that this is a very real danger in some circles. One of the deep concerns that has prompted me to write this book is a growing trend I have noticed—particularly among people committed to the biblical truth of God's sovereignty and divine election. Some of them flatly deny that God in any sense loves those whom He has not chosen for salvation.

I am convinced from Scripture that God is absolutely sovereign in the salvation of sinners. Salvation "does not depend on the man who wills or the man who runs, but on God who has mercy" (Rom. 9:16). We are redeemed not because of anything good in us, but because God chose us unto salvation. He chose certain individuals and passed over others, and He made that choice in eternity past, before the foundation of the world (Eph. 1:4). Moreover, He chose without regard to anything He foresaw in the elect; simply "according to the good pleasure of his will [and] to the praise of the glory of his grace" (vv. 5–6, KJV). Election arises from the love of God. Those whom He chose, He "loved . . . with an everlasting love [and drew them to Himself] with lovingkindness" (Jer. 31:3).

But certainly we can affirm those truths without also concluding that God's attitude toward the non-elect is one of utter hatred.

I am troubled by the tendency of some—often young people newly infatuated with Reformed doctrine—who insist that God cannot possibly love those who never repent and believe. I encounter this view, it seems, with increasing frequency. The argument inevitably goes like this: Psalm 7:11 tells us "God is angry with the wicked every day." It seems reasonable to assume that if God loved everyone, He would have chosen everyone unto salvation. Therefore, God does not love the non-elect. Those who hold this view often go to great lengths to argue that John 3:16 cannot really mean God loves the whole world.

Perhaps the best-known argument for this view is found in the unabridged edition of an otherwise excellent book, *The Sovereignty of God,* by A. W. Pink.[11] Pink wrote, "God loves whom He chooses. He does not love everybody."[12] Later in the book, he added this:

> Is it true that God *loves* the one who is *despising* and reject-ing His blessed Son? God is Light as well as Love, and therefore His love must be a *holy* love. To tell the Christ-rejecter that God loves him is to cauterize his conscience, as well as to afford him a sense of security in his sins. The fact is, that the love of God, is a truth for the saints only, and to present it to the enemies of God is to take the children's bread and cast it to the dogs. With the exception of John 3:16, not once in the four gospels do we read of the Lord Jesus—the perfect teacher—telling sinners that God loved them![13]

In an appendix to the unabridged edition, Pink argued that the word *world* in John 3:16 ("For God so loved the *world* . . . ") "refers to *the world of believers* (God's elect), in contradistinction from '*the world of the ungodly.*'"[14]

Pink was attempting to make the crucial point that God is sov-ereign in the exercise of His love. The gist of his argument is certainly valid: It is folly to think that God loves all alike, or that He is compelled by some rule of fairness to love everyone equally. Scripture teaches us that God loves because He chooses to love (cf. Deut. 7:6–7), because He is loving—because He is love (1 Jn. 4:8)—not because He is under some obligation to love everyone the same. Nothing but God's own sovereign good plea-sure compels Him to love sinners. Nothing but His own sovereign will governs His love. This has to be true, since there is certainly nothing in any sinner worthy of even the smallest degree of divine love.

Unfortunately, Pink took the corollary too far. The fact that some sinners are not elected to salvation is no proof that God's attitude toward them is utterly devoid of sincere love. We know from Scripture that God is compassionate, kind, generous, and good even to the most stubborn sinners. Who can deny that these mercies flow out of God's boundless love? Yet it is evident that they are showered even on unrepentant sinners. According to Paul, for example, the knowledge of divine goodness and forbearance and patience ought to lead sinners to repentance (Rom. 2:4). Yet the apostle acknowledged that many who are the recipients of these expressions of divine love spurn them and thereby store up wrath for themselves in the day of wrath (v. 5). The hardness of the sinful human heart is the only reason people persist in their sin, despite God's goodness to them. Is God therefore insincere when He pours forth mercies calling them to repentance? And how can anyone conclude that God's real attitude toward those who reject His mercies is nothing but sheer hatred?

I want to acknowledge, however, that explaining God's love toward the reprobate is not as simple as most modern evangelicals want to make it. Clearly there is a sense in which the psalmist's expression, "I hate the assembly of evildoers" (Ps. 26:5) is a reflection of the mind of God. "Do I not hate those who hate Thee, O Lord? And do I not loathe those who rise up against Thee? I hate them with the utmost hatred; they have become my enemies" (Ps. 139:21–22). Such hatred as the psalmist expressed is a virtue, and we have every reason to conclude that it is a hatred God Himself shares. After all, He *did* say, "I have hated Esau" (Mal. 1:3; Rom. 9:13). The context reveals God was speaking of a *whole race* of wicked people. So there is a true and real sense in which Scripture teaches that God hates the wicked.

Many try to dodge the difficulty this poses by suggesting that God hates the sin, not the sinner. Why, then does God condemn the sinner and consign the person—not merely the sin—to eternal hell? Clearly we cannot sweep the severity of this truth away by denying God's hatred for the wicked. Nor should we imagine that such hatred is any kind of blemish on the character of God. It is a holy hatred. It is perfectly consistent with His spotless, unapproachable, incomprehensible holiness.

God's Love for the Unbelieving World

YET I AM CONVINCED from Scripture that God's hatred toward the wicked is not a hatred undiluted by compassion, mercy, or love. We know from human experience that love and hatred are not mutually exclusive. It is not the least bit unusual to have concurrent feelings of love and hatred directed at the same person. We often speak of people who have love-hate relationships. There is no reason to deny that in an infinitely purer and more noble sense, God's hatred toward the wicked is accompanied by a sincere, compassionate love for them as well.[15]

The fact that God will send to eternal hell all sinners who persist in sin and unbelief proves His hatred toward them. On the other hand, the fact that God promises to forgive and bring into His eternal glory all who trust Christ as Savior—and even pleads with sinners to repent—proves His love toward them.

We must understand that it is God's very nature to love. The reason our Lord commanded us to love our enemies is "in order that you may be sons of your Father who is in heaven; for He causes His sun to rise on the evil and the good, and sends rain on the righteous and the unrighteous" (Matt. 5:45, NASB). That passage and the verses in its immediate context refute Arthur Pink's claim that Jesus never told sinners God loved them. Here Jesus clearly characterized His Father as One who loves even those who purposefully set themselves at enmity against Him.

While we are all eager to ask why a loving God lets bad things happen to His children, surely we should also ask why a holy

The God Who Loves

God lets good things happen to bad people. The answer is that God is merciful even to those who are not His own.

At this point, however, an important distinction must be made: God loves believers with a particular love. It is a family love, the ultimate love of an eternal Father for His children. It is the consummate love of a Bridegroom for His bride. It is an eternal love that guarantees their salvation from sin and its ghastly penalty. That special love is reserved for believers alone. Limiting this saving, everlasting love to His chosen ones does not render God's compassion, mercy, goodness, and love for the rest of mankind insincere or meaningless. When God invites sinners to repent and receive forgiveness (Isa. 1:18; Matt. 11:28–30) His pleading is from a sincere heart of genuine love. "'As I live!' declares the Lord God, 'I take no pleasure in the death of the wicked, but rather that the wicked turn from his way and live. Turn back, turn back from your evil ways! Why then will you die, O house of Israel?'" (Ezek. 33:11). Clearly God *does* love even those who spurn His tender mercy, but it is a different quality of love, and different in degree from His love for His own.

A parallel in the human realm would be this: I love my neighbors. I am commanded by numerous Scriptures to love them as I love myself (e.g., Lev. 19:18; Matt. 22:39; Lk. 10:29–37). I also love my wife. That, too, is in accord with Scripture (Eph. 5:25–28; Col. 3:19). But clearly my love for my wife is superior, both in excellence and in degree, to my love for my neighbor. I chose my wife; I did not choose my neighbor. I willingly brought my wife into my family to live with me for the rest of our lives. There's no reason to conclude that since I do not afford the same privilege to my neighbors, my love for them is not a real and genuine love. Likewise it is with God. He loves the elect in a special way reserved only for them. But that does not make His love for the rest of humanity any less real.

Furthermore, even in the human realm, love for one's spouse and love for one's neighbor still don't exhaust the different varieties

16

of love we share. I also love my children with the utmost fervency; yet again I love them with a different quality of love than my love for my wife. And I love my Christian neighbors in a way that rises above my love for my non-Christian neighbors. Obviously genuine love comes in varying kinds and degrees. Why is it difficult for us to conceive that God Himself loves different people differently and with different effects?

God's love for the elect is an infinite, eternal, saving love. We know from Scripture that this great love was the very cause of our election (Eph. 2:4). Such love clearly is not directed toward all of mankind indiscriminately, but is bestowed uniquely and individually on those whom God chose in eternity past.

But from that, it does not follow that God's attitude toward those He did not elect must be unmitigated hatred. Surely His pleading with the lost, His offers of mercy to the reprobate, and the call of the gospel to all who hear are all sincere expressions of the heart of a loving God. Remember, He has no pleasure in the death of the wicked, but tenderly calls sinners to turn from their evil ways and live. He freely offers the water of life to all (Isa. 55:1; Rev. 22:17). Those truths are not at all incompatible with the truth of divine sovereignty.

Reformed theology has historically been the branch of evangelicalism most strongly committed to the sovereignty of God. At the same time, the mainstream of Reformed theologians have always affirmed the love of God for all sinners. John Calvin himself wrote regarding John 3:16, "[Two] points are distinctly stated to us: namely, that faith in Christ brings life to all, and that Christ brought life, because the Father loves the human race, and wishes that they should not perish."[16] Calvin went on to add this:

> [In John 3:16 the evangelist] has employed the universal
> term *whosoever*, both to invite all indiscriminately to partake
> of life, and to cut off every excuse from unbelievers. Such is
> also the import of the term *world*, which he formerly used; for

though nothing will be found in *the world* that is worthy of the favor of God, yet he shows himself to be reconciled to the whole world, when he invites all without exception to the faith of Christ, which is nothing else than an entrance into life.

Let us remember, on the other hand, that while *life* is promised universally to *all who believe* in Christ, still faith is not common to all, but the elect alone are they whose eyes God opens, that they may seek him by faith.[17]

Calvin's comments are both balanced and biblical. He points out that both the gospel invitation and "the world" that God loves are by no means limited to the elect alone. But he also recognizes that God's electing, saving love is uniquely bestowed on His chosen ones.

These same truths have been vigorously defended by a host of Reformed stalwarts, including Thomas Boston, John Brown, Andrew Fuller, W. G. T. Shedd, R. L. Dabney, B. B. Warfield, John Murray, R. B. Kuiper, and many others.[18] In no sense does belief in divine sovereignty rule out the love of God for all humanity.

We're seeing today an almost unprecedented interest in the doctrines of the Reformation and the Puritan era. I'm very encouraged by this in most respects. A return to these historic truths is, I'm convinced, absolutely necessary if the church is to survive. Yet there is a danger when overzealous souls misuse a doctrine like divine sovereignty to deny God's sincere offer of mercy to all sinners.

We must maintain a carefully balanced perspective as we pursue our study of God's love. God's love cannot be isolated from His wrath and vice versa. Nor are His love and wrath in opposition to each other like some mystical yin-yang principle. Both attributes are constant, perfect, without ebb or flow. God Himself is immutable—unchanging. He is not loving one moment and wrathful the next. His wrath coexists with His love; therefore, the two never contradict. Such are the perfections of God that we can never begin to comprehend these things. Above all, we must not set them against one another, as if there were somehow a discrepancy in God. God is always true to Himself and true to His Word (Rom. 3:4; 2 Tim. 2:13).

Both God's wrath and His love work to the same ultimate end—His glory. God is glorified in the condemnation of the wicked, and He is glorified in the salvation of His people. The expression of His wrath and the expression of His love are both necessary to display His full glory. Since His glory is the great design of His eternal plan, and since all that He has revealed about Himself is essential to His glory, we must not ignore any aspect of His character. We cannot magnify His love to the exclusion of the other attributes.

Nevertheless, those who truly know God will testify that the deepest spiritual delights are derived from the knowledge of His love. His love is what drew us to Him in the first place: "We love him, because he first loved us" (1 Jn. 4:19, KJV). His love—certainly not anything worthy in us—is the reason He saved us and bestowed on us such rich spiritual privileges: "But God, being rich in mercy, *because of His great love with which He loved us,* even when we were dead in our transgressions, made us alive together with Christ (by grace you have been saved), and raised us up with Him, and seated us with Him in the heavenly places, in Christ Jesus" (Eph. 2:4–6, emphasis added).

We will return again and again to some of these same truths as we pursue our study in this book. My purpose is not to engage in polemics. My only design is to present God's love in such a fashion that the splendor of it will fill your heart. If you are a Christian, my prayer is that the glory and greatness of His love will deepen your love for Him, and that you will grasp the joys and pains of life with a correct understanding of God's love.

If you are not a believer, perhaps God is drawing you to Himself. We know from Scripture that He is calling you to repentance and offering you the water of life. My prayer is that as you read these pages, the wonder and privilege of divine love will be unfolded to you—and that you will therefore respond to the truth of God's Word with a humble and believing heart. I encourage you to drink in the mercy that Jesus offered in these tender words: "Come to Me, all who are weary and heavy-laden, and I will give you rest. Take My yoke upon you, and learn from Me, for I am gentle and humble in heart; and you shall find rest for your souls. For My yoke is easy, and My load is light" (Matt. 11:28–30).

But be warned: the knowledge of God's goodness and mercy will only deepen your condemnation if you spurn Him. "How shall we escape if we neglect so great a salvation?" (Heb. 2:3). God's love is a refuge for repentant sinners only. Those satisfied with their sin should take no solace from the knowledge that God is full of mercy and compassion. And impenitent sinners inclined to disregard the Savior's offer of mercy should first consider this crucial warning of Scripture: "If we go on sinning willfully after receiving the knowledge of the truth, there no longer remains a sacrifice for sins, but a certain terrifying expectation of judgment, and the fury of a fire which will consume the adversaries" (Heb. 10:26–27).

That "terrifying expectation of judgment, and the fury of a fire which will consume the adversaries" provide the only legitimate context in which anyone can justly apprehend God's love.

> I will extol Thee, my God, O King;
> And I will bless Thy name forever and ever.
> Every day I will bless Thee,
> And I will praise Thy name forever and ever.
> Great is the Lord, and highly to be praised;
> And His greatness is unsearchable.
> One generation shall praise Thy works to another,
> And shall declare Thy mighty acts.
> On the glorious splendor of Thy majesty,
> And on Thy wonderful works, I will meditate.
> And men shall speak of the power of Thine awesome acts;
> And I will tell of Thy greatness.

They shall eagerly utter the memory of Thine abundant goodness,
And shall shout joyfully of Thy righteousness.
The Lord is gracious and merciful;
Slow to anger and great in lovingkindness.
The Lord is good to all,
And His mercies are over all His works.
All Thy works shall give thanks to Thee, O Lord,
And Thy godly ones shall bless Thee.
They shall speak of the glory of Thy kingdom,
And talk of Thy power;
To make known to the sons of men Thy mighty acts,
And the glory of the majesty of Thy kingdom.
Thy kingdom is an everlasting kingdom,
And Thy dominion endures throughout all generations.
The Lord sustains all who fall,
And raises up all who are bowed down.
The eyes of all look to Thee,
And Thou dost give them their food in due time.
Thou dost open Thy hand,
And dost satisfy the desire of every living thing.
The Lord is righteous in all His ways,
And kind in all His deeds.
The Lord is near to all who call upon Him,
To all who call upon Him in truth.
He will fulfill the desire of those who fear Him;
He will also hear their cry and will save them.
The Lord keeps all who love Him;
But all the wicked, He will destroy.
My mouth will speak the praise of the Lord;
And all flesh will bless His holy name forever and ever.

—Psalm 145 (emphasis added)

"May the Lord direct your hearts into the love of God"
(2 Thess. 3:5).

21

God Is Love

Love Is at the Heart of God's Character

Everyone Who Loves Is Born of God and Knows God

The One Who Does Not Love Does Not Know God

The Cross Is the Consummate Proof of Divine Love

Chapter 2

God Is Love

On a cross-country domestic airliner a few years ago, I plugged in the earphones and began to listen to the music program. I was amazed at how much of the music dealt with love. At the time I was preaching through 1 John 4, so the subject of love was very much on my mind. I couldn't help noticing how glib and shallow most of the lyrics were. "She Loves You, Yeah, Yeah, Yeah" is a classic by worldly standards. But few people would argue that its lyrics are truly profound.

I began to realize how easily our culture trivializes love by sentimentalizing it. The love we hear about in popular songs is almost always portrayed as a *feeling*—usually involving unfulfilled desire. Most love songs describe love as a longing, a passion, a craving that is never quite satisfied, a set of expectations that are never met. Unfortunately, that sort of love is devoid of any ultimate meaning. It is actually a tragic reflection of human lostness.

As I thought about it, I realized something else: Most love songs not only reduce love to an emotion, but they also make it an involuntary one. People "fall" in love. They get swept off their feet by love. They can't help themselves. They go crazy for love.

One song laments, "I'm hooked on a feeling," while another confesses, "I think I'm going out of my head."

It may seem a nice romantic sentiment to characterize love as uncontrollable passion, but those who think carefully about it will realize that such "love" is both selfish and irrational. It is far from the biblical concept of love. Love, according to Scripture, is not a helpless sensation of desire. Rather, it is a purposeful act of self-giving. The one who genuinely loves is deliberately devoted to the one loved. True love arises from the will—not from blind emotion. Consider, for example, this description of love from the pen of the apostle Paul:

> Love is patient, love is kind, and is not jealous; love does not brag and is not arrogant, does not act unbecomingly; it does not seek its own, is not provoked, does not take into account a wrong suffered, does not rejoice in unrighteousness, but rejoices with the truth; bears all things, believes all things, hopes all things, endures all things (1 Cor. 13:4–7).

That kind of love cannot possibly be an emotion that ebbs and flows involuntarily. It is not a mere feeling. All the attributes of love Paul lists involve the mind and volition. In other words, the love he describes is a thoughtful, willing commitment. Also, notice that genuine love "does not seek its own." That means if I truly love, I'm concerned not with having my desires filled, but with seeking the best for whoever is the object of my love.

So the mark of true love is not unbridled desire or wild passion; it is a giving of oneself. Jesus Himself underscored this when He told His disciples, "Greater love has no one than this, that one lay down his life for his friends" (Jn. 15:13). If love is a giving of oneself, then the greatest love is shown by laying down one's very life. And of course, such love was perfectly modeled by Christ.

God Is Love

Love Is at the Heart of God's Character

THE APOSTLE JOHN has been called "the apostle of love" because he wrote so much on the subject. He was fascinated by it, overwhelmed with the reality that he was loved by God. He often referred to himself in his gospel as "the disciple whom Jesus loved" (Jn. 21:20; cf. 13:23; 20:2; 21:7).

In his first epistle, John wrote, "God is love. By this the love of God was manifested in us, that God has sent His only begotten Son into the world so that we might live through Him" (1 Jn. 4:8–9). Those words are a clear echo of a familiar passage, John 3:16: "For God so loved the world, that He gave His only begotten Son, that whoever believes in Him should not perish, but have eternal life."

Look carefully, first of all, at this simple phrase from 1 John 4:8: "God is love."

In what sense is it true that God is love? There are many ways to *misunderstand* John's meaning. In fact, 1 John 4:8 seems a particular favorite of cultists. All kinds of false sects from Christian Science to the Children of God have misapplied this verse to support wildly heretical notions—the former using it to portray "God as divine Principle, Love, rather than personality";[1] and the latter using it to justify sexual promiscuity.[2] It is important that we understand and reject not only those doctrines, but also the false ideas on which they are based, lest we be led astray in our own thinking.

First, the expression "God is love" is not meant to depersonalize God or portray Him as a force, a sensation, a principle, or some sort of cosmic energy. He is a personal Being, with all the attributes of personality—volition, feeling, and intellect. In fact, what the apostle is saying is that God's love is the highest expression of His person. Therefore, to use this text to attempt to depersonalize God is to do great violence to the clear meaning of Scripture. Such an interpretation actually turns this text on its head.

Second, this verse by no means identifies God with everything our society labels love. Gordon Clark wrote, "John is not saying that all sorts of emotions called love are from God. The romanticism of Goethe, and much more the present sexual debauchery, are not from God."[3] In fact, those who cite this verse to attempt to legitimize illicit forms of "love" are about as far from the apostle's intent as it is possible to get. The love of which he speaks is a pure and holy love, consistent with all the divine attributes.

Third, this is not meant to be a definition of God or a summary of His attributes. Divine love in no way minimizes or nullifies God's other attributes—His omniscience, His omnipotence, His omnipresence, His immutability, His lordship, His righteousness, His wrath against sin, or any of His glorious perfections. Deny any one of them and you have denied the God of Scripture.

There is certainly more to God than love. Similar expressions elsewhere in Scripture demonstrate this. For example, the same apostle who penned these words also wrote, "God is Spirit" (Jn. 4:24). We have already noted that Scripture also says, "God is a consuming fire" (Deut. 4:24; Heb. 12:29). And Psalm 7:11 says, "God is a righteous judge, and a God who has indignation every day." The simple statement "God is love" obviously does not convey everything that can be known about God. We know from Scripture that He is also holy and righteous and true to His Word. God's love does not contradict His holiness; instead, it complements and magnifies it and gives it its deepest meaning. So we cannot isolate this one phrase from the rest of Scripture and attempt to make love represent the sum of what we know about God.

Notice, by the way, that this phrase "God is love" is not even the only such statement in John's first epistle

In the introduction to the epistle, at the very outset, John gave this shorthand statement of the message he wanted to declare: "That *God is light,* and in Him there is no darkness at all" (1 Jn. 1:5, emphasis added). When the apostle says, "God is light," he encompasses several ideas, including holiness, truth, and divine splendor. So as we read from this epistle, remember that these two statements, "God is light" and "God is love," must be kept in balance at all times. God is love, but having said that, we have not said everything that is true about God.

Nevertheless, we dare not minimize the force of this crucial text. By saying "God is love," the apostle is making a very strong statement about the character and the essence of God. It is God's very nature to love—love permeates who He is. Or, as John Stott has written, "God is love in His innermost being."[4] Stott calls the apostle's declaration that God is love "the most comprehensive and sublime of all biblical affirmations about God's being."[5]

This statement, "God is love," is so profound that no less than Augustine saw it as an important evidence for the doctrine of the Trinity. If God is love—that is, if love is intrinsic to His very nature—then He has always loved, even from eternity past, before there was any created object for His love. Augustine suggested that this love must have existed between the Persons of the Trinity, with the Father loving the Son, and so on. So according to Augustine, the very fact that God is love corroborates the doctrine of the Trinity.

Clearly the love this text describes is an eternal reality. It flows from the very nature of God and is not a response to anything outside the person of God. The apostle does not say, "God is *loving,*" as if he were speaking of one of many divine attributes, but "God is *love*"—as if to say that love pervades and influences all His attributes.

For example, we know that God is holy, "undefiled, separated from sinners and exalted above the heavens," (Heb. 7:26). As a holy being, He would be perfectly righteous to view all sinners with the utmost contempt. But His is a loving holiness that reaches out to sinners with salvation for them—the antithesis of aloofness or indifference.

Love surely tempers even God's judgments. What a wonder it is that He who is a consuming fire, He who is unapproachable light, is also the personification of love! He postpones His judgments against sin while pleading with sinners to repent. He freely offers mercy to all who *will* repent. He shows longsuffering and goodness even to many who steel their hearts against Him. Divine love not only keeps divine wrath in check while God appeals to the sinner—but it also proves that God is just when He finally condemns.

And even when He condemns, "God is love." Our God therefore shows Himself to be not only glorious but also good; not only spotlessly holy, but also wondrously compassionate; not only righteous, but also a God of matchless love. And that love emanates from His very essence.

Everyone Who Loves Is Born of God and Knows God

FROM THE TRUTH that God is love, the apostle draws this corollary: "Love is from God" (1 Jn. 4:7). God is the source of all true love. Love is therefore the best evidence that a person truly knows God: "Everyone who loves is born of God and knows God. The one who does not love does not know God" (vv. 7–8). In other words, love is the proof of a regenerate heart. Only true Christians are capable of genuine love.

Clearly, the kind of love the apostle is speaking of is a higher, purer form of love than we commonly know from human experience. The love of which he speaks does not flow naturally from the human heart. It is not a carnal love, a romantic love, or even a familial love. It is a supernatural love that is peculiar to those who know God. It is *godly* love.

In fact, the apostle employed a Greek word for "love" that was highly unusual in first-century culture. The word was *agape,* not a common word until the New Testament made it so. When a typical first-century pagan thought of love, *agape* was not the word that would have come to mind. In fact, there were two other common Greek words for love: *phileo,* to describe brotherly love, and *eros,* to describe everything from romantic love to sexual passion.

Phileo is occasionally used as a synonym for *agape,* but generally the word *agape* is used as a more refined and elevated term. In the sense that John uses it here, *agape* is unique to God. He is the sole source of it.

Love for one's family, romantic love, and the love of good friends all fall into the category of what Scripture calls "natural affection" (Rom. 1:31; 2 Tim. 3:3, KJV). Even these expressions of "natural affection," or human love, can be marvelously rich. They fill life with color and joy. They are, however, merely pale reflections of the image of God in His creatures. His love is *perfect* love. It is that pure, holy, godly love which can be known only by those who are born of Him. It is the same unfathomable love that moved God to send "His only begotten Son into the world so that we might live through Him" (1 Jn. 4:9).

Donald W. Burdick gives three characteristics of this godly sort of love:

> *It is spontaneous.* There was nothing of value in the persons loved that called forth such sacrificial love. God of His own free will set His love on us in spite of our enmity and sin. *[Agape]* is love that is initiated by the lover because he wills to love, not because of the value or lovableness of the person loved. *It is self-giving. [Agape]* is not interested in what it can gain, but in what it can give. It is not bent on satisfying the lover, but on helping the one loved whatever the cost. *It is active. [Agape]* is not mere sentiment cherished in the heart. Nor is it mere words however eloquent. It does involve feeling and may express itself in words, but it is primarily an attitude toward another that moves the will to act in helping to meet the need of the one loved.[6]

All true believers have this love; and all who have it are true believers.

This kind of love cannot be conjured up by the human will. It is wrought in the hearts of believers by God Himself. "We love, because He first loved us" (1 Jn. 4:19). Love for God and love for fellow believers is an inevitable result of the new birth, by which we "become partakers of the divine nature" (2 Pet. 1:4). Just as it is God's nature to love, love is characteristic of His true children. "The love of God has been poured out within our hearts through the Holy Spirit who was given to us" (Rom. 5:5).

Godly love, therefore, is one of the most important tests of the reality of one's faith.

The One Who Does Not Love Does Not Know God

IT IS IMPORTANT to understand the context of John's first epistle. He is writing about assurance of salvation and outlining several practical and doctrinal tests that either demonstrate or disprove the genuineness of one's salvation.

John is writing to help struggling believers gain assurance. He says so in 1 John 5:13: "These things I have written to you who believe in the name of the Son of God, *in order that you may know that you have eternal life*" (emphasis added).

But along the way he has a secondary purpose, and that is to destroy the *false assurance* of those who may profess faith in Christ without really knowing Him. Therefore, he writes such things as, "If we say that we have fellowship with Him and yet walk in the darkness, we lie and do not practice the truth" (1:6). And, "The one who says, 'I have come to know Him,' and does not keep His commandments, is a liar, and the truth is not in him" (2:4). And, "The one who says he is in the light and yet hates his brother is in the darkness until now" (v. 9).

Here he makes godly love a kind of litmus test for the true

Christian: "The one who does not love does not know God, for God is love" (4:8). With regard to that statement, Martyn Lloyd-Jones observed,

> John does not put this merely as an exhortation. He puts it in such a way that it becomes a desperately serious matter, and I almost tremble as I proclaim this doctrine. There are people who are unloving, unkind, always criticizing, whispering, backbiting, pleased when they hear something against another Christian. Oh, my heart grieves and bleeds for them as I think of them; they are pronouncing and proclaiming that they are not born of God. They are outside the life of God; and I repeat, there is no hope for such people unless they repent and turn to Him.[7]

Sadly, most of us have encountered professing Christians whose hearts seem bereft of any genuine love. The apostle John's admonition is a solemn reminder that a mere pretension of faith in Christ is worthless. *Genuine* faith will inevitably be shown by love. After all, real faith works through love (Gal. 5:6).

This sort of God-given love is not easily counterfeited. Look at all that is involved: love for God Himself (1 Cor. 16:22); love for the brethren (1 Jn. 3:14); love of truth and righteousness (Rom. 6:17–18); love for the Word of God (Psa. 1:2); and even love for one's enemies! (Matt. 5:44). Such love is contrary to human nature. It is antithetical to our natural selfishness. The very thought of loving those things is odious to the sinful heart.

Later in this same chapter, the apostle writes, "God is love, and the one who abides in love abides in God, and God abides in him" (v. 16)—again making the godly kind of love the mark of genuine faith.

Martyn Lloyd-Jones listed ten simple, practical ways of knowing whether we abide in love.[8] I've paraphrased them here and added Scripture references to underscore each point:

❏ Is there a loss of the sense that God is against me? (Rom. 5:1; 8:31).

❏ Is there a loss of craven fear of God, and a corresponding increase in godly fear? (cf. 1 Jn. 4:18; Heb. 12:28).

❏ Do I sense the love of God for me? (1 Jn. 4:16).

❏ Do I know that my sins are forgiven? (Rom. 4:7–8).

❏ Do I have a sense of gratitude to God? (Col. 2:6–7).

❏ Do I have an increasing hatred for sin? (Rom. 7:15–16).

❏ Do I desire to please God and live a holy life? (Jn. 14:21; 1 Jn. 2:5–6).

❏ Is there a desire to know God better and draw near to Him? (Phil. 3:10).

❏ Is there a conscious regret that my love for Him is less than what it ought to be? (Phil. 1:9–10).

❏ Is there a sense of delight in hearing about God and the things of God? (Ps. 1:1–2).

Suppose you fail those tests. How can you know the love of God? In Lloyd-Jones's words, "You need not start traveling the mystic way, you need not try to work up feelings; there is only one thing for you to do: face God, see yourself and your sin, and see Christ as your Saviour."[9]

The Cross Is the Consummate Proof of Divine Love

LET'S NOW TAKE A FRESH LOOK at the text from which we drew the title of this chapter: "God is love. By this the love of God was manifested in us, that God has sent His only begotten Son into the world so that we might live through Him" (1 Jn. 4:8–9).

We would not be doing justice to this verse if we limited our discussion of divine love to abstract terms. The love of God is not merely a subjective noumenon. It is dynamic, active, vibrant, and powerful. God has "manifested" His love, or displayed it in a particular act that can be examined objectively.

In other words, Scripture does not merely say "God is love" and leave it to the individual to interpret subjectively what that means. There is a very important doctrinal context in which the love of God is explained and illustrated. To affirm that God is love while denying the doctrine underlying and defining that truth is to render the truth itself meaningless.

But that is precisely what many have done. For example, our adversaries, the theological liberals, are very keen to affirm that God is love; yet they often flatly deny the significance of Christ's substitutionary atonement. They suggest that because God is love, Christ did not actually need to die as a substitutionary sacrifice to turn away the divine wrath from sinners. They portray God as easy to mollify, and they characterize the death of Christ as an act of martyrdom or a moral example for believers—denying that it was God's own wrath that needed to be propitiated through a blood sacrifice, and denying that He purposely gave His Son in order to make such an atonement. Thus, they reject the consummate manifestation of God's love, even while attempting to make divine love the centerpiece of their system.

I commonly encounter people who think that because God is love, theology doesn't really matter. A young man recently wrote me a letter that said in part, "Do you really think God is concerned about all the points of doctrine that divide us Christians? How much better it would be if we forgot our doctrinal differences and just showed the world the love of God!"

But that position is untenable, because many who call themselves Christians are deceivers. For that reason the apostle John began the chapter from which our text is taken with these words:

"Beloved, do not believe every spirit, but test the spirits to see whether they are from God; because many false prophets have gone out into the world" (1 Jn. 4:1).

And since an important body of doctrine underlies what Scripture teaches about divine love, it is a fallacy to think of divine love and sound theology as in any way opposed to each other.

Martyn Lloyd-Jones wrote about this very thing:

> The great tendency in this present century has been to put up as antitheses the idea of God as a God of love on the one side, and theology or dogma or doctrine on the other. Now the average person has generally taken up such a position as follows: "You know, I am not interested in your doctrine. Surely the great mistake the church has made throughout the centuries is all this talk about dogma, all this doctrine of sin, and the doctrine of the Atonement, and this idea of justification and sanctification. Of course there are some people who may be interested in that kind of thing; they may enjoy reading and arguing about it, but as for myself," says this man, "there does not seem to be any truth in it; all I say is that God is love." So he puts up this idea of God as love over and against all these doctrines which the church has taught throughout the centuries.[10]

Indeed, such thinking has been the predominant mood both in popular thinking and in much of organized religion for the bulk of this century. That mindset in many ways has become the hallmark of the visible church in the twentieth century.

Lloyd-Jones points out that according to 1 John 4:9–10, "people who thus put up as opposites the idea of God as love and these basic, fundamental doctrines can, in the last analysis, *know nothing whatsoever about the love of God.*"[11]

Indeed, looking at these verses again, we discover that the apostle explains the love of God in terms of sacrifice, atonement for sin, and propitiation: "In this is love, not that we loved God, but that He loved us and sent His Son to be the *propitiation* for our sins" (1 Jn. 4:10, emphasis added). That word speaks of a sacrifice designed to turn away the wrath of an offended deity. What the apostle is saying is that God gave His Son as an offering for sin, to satisfy His own wrath and justice in the salvation of sinners.

This is the very heart of the gospel. The "good news" is not that God is willing to overlook sin and forgive sinners. That would compromise God's holiness. That would leave justice unfulfilled. That would trample on true righteousness. Furthermore, that would not be love on God's part, but apathy.

The *real* good news is that God Himself, through the sacrifice of His Son, paid the price of sin. He took the initiative ("not that we loved God, but that He loved us"). He was not responding to anything in sinners that made them worthy of His grace. On the contrary, His love was altogether undeserved by sinful humanity. The sinners for whom Christ died were worthy of nothing but His wrath. As Paul wrote, "Christ died for the *ungodly*. For one will hardly die for a righteous man; though perhaps for the good man someone would dare even to die. But God demonstrates His own love toward us, in that *while we were yet sinners,* Christ died for us" (Rom. 5:7–8, emphasis added).

Because God is righteous, He must punish sin; He cannot simply absolve guilt and leave justice unsatisfied. But the death of Christ totally satisfied God's justice, His righteousness, and His holy hatred of sin.

Some people recoil at the thought of an innocent victim making atonement for guilty sinners. They like the idea that people should pay for their own sins. But take away this doctrine of substitutionary atonement and you have no gospel at all. If the death of Christ was anything less than a guilt offering for sinners, no one could ever be saved.

But in Christ's death on the cross, there is the highest possible expression of divine love. He, who *is* love, sent His precious Son to die as an atonement for sin. If your sense of fair play is outraged by that—good! It ought to be shocking. It ought to be astonishing. It ought to stagger you. Think it through, and you'll begin to get a picture of the enormity of the price God paid to manifest His love.

The cross of Christ also gives the most complete and accurate perspective on an issue we will revisit again and again in this book: the balance between God's love and His wrath.

At the cross His *love* is shown to sinful humanity—fallen creatures who have no rightful claim on His goodness, His mercy, or His love. And His *wrath* is poured out on His beloved Son, who had done nothing worthy of any kind of punishment.

If you're not awestruck by that, then you don't yet understand it.

If you do catch a glimpse of this truth, however, your thoughts of God as a loving Father will take on a whole new depth and richness. "God is love"—and He demonstrated His love for us in that while we were sinners in rebellion against Him, He gave His only Son to die on our behalf—and so that we might live through Him (Rom. 5:8; 1 Jn. 4:9–10). That is the very heart of the gospel, and it holds forth the only hope to those in bondage to their sin: "Believe in the Lord Jesus, and you shall be saved" (Acts 16:31).

Behold the Goodness . . .

Sin City

A Reluctant Prophet and a Great Revival

God's Gift of Repentance

Chapter 3

Behold the Goodness . . .

A. W. TOZER WROTE, "What comes into our minds when we think about God is the most important thing about us."[1] Tozer was right. A proper conception of God provides the foundation of all that is absolutely essential to spiritual life and health. On the other hand, for those with a seriously distorted concept of who God is, genuine faith is utterly impossible. Therefore, to misconstrue God's character can even be spiritually fatal.

That is the real danger posed by the contemporary misunderstanding of God's love. In spite of the clarity of Scripture on God's love, millions are kept in spiritual darkness by a notion of God that is completely out of balance. They want a God who is loving but not wrathful. The God of Scripture doesn't fit the bill. They therefore worship a god of their own making. Their thoughts about God constitute sheer idolatry.

For this very reason there is an inherent danger in focusing too intently on any one attribute of God, such as His love. The apostle Paul wrote, "Behold therefore the goodness *and* severity of God" (Rom. 11:22, KJV, emphasis added). It is crucial that we maintain the biblical balance in our thinking. While we study God's love, we must bear in mind that God is also holy, innocent, undefiled, separated from sinners, exalted above the heavens (Heb. 7:26); that He "is a righteous judge, and a God who has indignation every day" (Ps. 7:11); and that "if a man does not repent, He will sharpen His sword; He has bent His bow and made it ready. He has also prepared for Himself deadly weapons; He makes His arrows fiery shafts" (vv. 12–13). "For our God is a consuming fire" (Heb. 12:29). He is a jealous God, visiting the iniquity of the fathers on the children, on the third and the fourth generations of those who hate Him (Exod. 20:5; Deut. 5:9).

God's love, measureless as it is, does not negate any of those truths. We must not stress divine love to the extent that we distort these other equally crucial truths about God. Unfortunately, that is precisely the tragic path our culture as a whole has taken. God's wrath is virtually a taboo subject. Most people would be only too willing to relegate the notion of divine wrath to the scrap heap of outmoded or unsophisticated religious ideas. There is no room for an angry God in an "enlightened" age such as ours. Even some preachers who profess to believe Scripture, yet knowing how people feel about an angry God, are careful to avoid such themes in favor of a friendlier message. All of this has only intensified the problem.

One widespread misconception is that the angry-God concept is confined to the Old Testament. According to this view, Scripture reveals God to us progressively. The Old Testament portrayed Him as a wrathful, angry deity—but only to accommodate the primitive understanding of our ancient forefathers. Supposedly the New Testament—and particularly Jesus—corrected this "faulty" concept, emphasizing the love of God. Those who hold this view suggest that the loving God of the New Testament reflects a more sophisticated understanding of God than the patriarchs had.

There is one serious problem with that theory: all the biblical data quite clearly refute it. For one thing, the Old Testament has as much to say about the love of God as the New. Again and again the Old Testament exalts the lovingkindness and goodness of God. In fact, the word for "lovingkindness" is applied to God more than 150 times in the Old Testament alone: "The Lord's lovingkindnesses indeed never cease, for His compassions never fail. They are new every morning; great is Thy faithfulness" (Lam. 3:22–23). That truth is emphasized from the beginning to the end of the Old Testament.

God's love for Israel is revealed over and over, in spite of Israel's rejection. The depiction of that love in the prophecy of Hosea is unmistakable, and even shocking. Hosea became a living illustration of divine love in his relationship with his wife, Gomer. She became a prostitute and bore several illegitimate children. She shattered her husband's heart. She pursued her life of adulterous harlotries until she was totally dissolute. Finally, she was placed for sale in a slave market. Hosea had followed her wretched career, and behind the scenes he made sure her needs were met. When she was placed on the block to be sold, he bought her for his own, took her home, and treated her as if she were a virgin. Hosea's laudable, generous, forgiving love for his evil wife, and his willingness to take her back no matter what she had done, are object lessons to illustrate God's love for sinning Israel. Hosea cites God's own plea to that wayward nation: "My heart is turned over within Me, all My compassions are kindled" (Hos. 11.8). How faithfully He loves!

Throughout the Old Testament God is portrayed in this manner, as a God of tender mercies, infinite lovingkindness, great compassion, and patient longsuffering.

Just to keep the record straight, the New Testament has as much to say about the *wrath* of God as the Old. It was Jesus Himself, in the New Testament, who gave the fullest and most explicit descriptions of the horrors of hell (Matt. 5:29–30; Mk. 9:43–48; Lk. 16:19–31). And the New Testament also records these words of Jesus: "But I will warn you whom to fear: fear the One who after He has killed has authority to cast into hell; yes, I tell you, fear Him!" (Lk. 12:5). The final New Testament description of Christ in His Second-Coming glory says, "From His mouth comes a sharp sword, so that with it He may smite the nations; and He will rule them with a rod of iron; and He treads the wine press of the fierce wrath of God, the Almighty" (Rev. 19:15).

So there is absolutely no basis for the notion that the New Testament changes the concept of God from wrathful to loving. The same God reveals Himself to us in both Testaments. The glorious truth is that "God is love" (1 Jn. 4:8, 16)—yet it is nevertheless "a terrifying thing to fall into the hands of the living God" (Heb. 10:31). Both truths are stressed in both Testaments.

One further clarification needs to be made on this point. When we speak of God's love and God's wrath, we are not talking about anything like human passions. According to the best-known Protestant confession of faith, God is "a most pure spirit, invisible, without body, parts, or passions, immutable. . . ."[2] God's wrath and His love are fixed and steady dispositions. They are not moods or passionate emotions. He does not swing wildly from one temperament to the other. To think of God that way is to deny that He is eternally unchanging. He Himself says: "I, the Lord, do not change" (Mal. 3:6). With God "there is no variation, or shifting shadow" (Jas. 1:17). He is "the same the same yesterday and today, yes and forever" (Heb. 13:8).

Nor do God's wrath and love imply any contradiction in His nature. "He cannot deny Himself" (2 Tim. 2:13). His wrath is not inconsistent with His love. Because He so completely loves what is true and right, He must hate all that is false and wrong. Because He so perfectly loves His children, He seeks what blesses and edifies them, and hates all that curses and debases them. Therefore, His wrath against sin is actually an expression of His love for His people. His chastening for their sin is proof that He is a loving Father (Heb. 12:6–11). And when He exercises vengeance against the enemies of truth, that also reveals His love for His chosen ones. Israel's history is filled with examples of these truths.

One classic example of this was Nineveh, a city that was Israel's nemesis for several centuries. There both the goodness and the severity of God were dramatically put on display. In fact, nowhere are God's lovingkindness and His holy wrath seen side by side more vividly than in the history of Nineveh. In this chapter we will examine God's goodness to the city, and in the chapter that follows we will see how that goodness finally gave way to an awful outpouring of divine wrath.

Sin City

NINEVEH WAS AN ancient city founded by Nimrod. Genesis 10:8–12 records that Nimrod founded the entire Babylonian kingdom, of which Nineveh was a part (cf. Mic. 5:6). Nimrod's Babylon became the source of virtually every false religious system.[3] That is why Scripture makes reference to "Babylon the great, the mother of harlots and of the abominations of the Earth" (Rev. 17:5). From its very beginning, Nineveh was one of the most important cities of the Babylonian empire, steeped in wickedness and debauchery. Nineveh opposed everything the true God stood for and vice versa.

In the eighth century B.C., Nineveh became the capital of Assyria. The Assyrians were known for their wicked ruthlessness. One author says,

> These people ruled with hideous tyranny and violence from the Caucasus and the Caspian to the Persian Gulf, and from beyond the Tigris to Asia Minor and Egypt. The Assyrian kings literally tormented the world. They flung away the bodies of soldiers like so much clay; they made pyramids of human heads; they sacrificed holocausts of the sons and daughters of their enemies; they burned cities; they filled populous lands with death and devastation;

they reddened broad deserts with carnage of warriors; they scattered whole countries with the corpses of their defenders as with chaff; they impaled 'heaps of men' on stakes, and strewed the mountains and choked the rivers with dead bones; they cut off the hands of kings, and nailed them on the walls, and left their bodies to rot with bears and dogs on the entrance gates of cities; they cut down warriors like weeds, or smote them like wild beasts in the forests, and covered pillars with the flayed skins of rival monarchs . . . and these things they did without sentiment or compunction.[4]

Nineveh represented the seat of this evil culture. Understandably, the Israelites hated Nineveh and all that the Assyrians represented.

A Reluctant Prophet and a Great Revival

AT THE VERY HEIGHT of Assyrian power, God commanded a prophet of Israel to go to Nineveh and warn the people there of God's impending judgment. Not surprisingly, the prophet rebelled.

That prophet was Jonah, whose history is familiar to every Sunday school student. Commanded by God to go to Nineveh, Jonah boarded a ship in the Mediterranean—and headed the opposite direction! (Jonah 1:3). "The Lord hurled a great wind on the sea . . . so that the ship was about to break up" (v. 4). The sailors on the ship discovered that Jonah had angered God, and on Jonah's own instructions they threw him overboard (vv. 12–15).

God had prepared a great fish to be at precisely the right spot, and the fish swallowed Jonah (v. 17). After three days and nights in the fish's belly—time spent by the disobedient prophet praying one of the finest prayers of repentance recorded in Scripture—Jonah was miraculously spared (2:1–9). "The Lord commanded the fish, and it vomited Jonah up onto the dry land" (2:10).

Scripture says, "Now the word of the Lord came to Jonah the second time, saying, 'Arise, go to Nineveh the great city and proclaim to it the proclamation which I am going to tell you'" (3:1–2). This time, albeit still reluctantly, "Jonah arose and went to Nineveh according to the word of the Lord" (v. 3).

Have you ever noticed *why* Jonah attempted to flee Nineveh? It was not because he feared the city's inhabitants. It was not that he was intimidated by the thought of preaching God's Word to pagans. Nothing indicated that Jonah was the least bit timid in the face of the Lord's enemies. In fact, what little we know about him proves he was not a particularly shy man.

Jonah was very candid about why he fled his duty. This was the explanation he gave God: "I knew that Thou art a gracious and compassionate God, slow to anger and abundant in lovingkindness, and one who relents concerning calamity" (4:2). In short, because he knew God loves sinners and seeks to save them, Jonah did not want to warn the Gentile Ninevites. He preferred to keep silent and allow God's judgment to take them by surprise. He would have been happiest if God had wiped the Ninevites from the face of the earth without any warning. His worst fear was that the city would repent, and then God would forestall His judgment.

That is, in fact, precisely what happened. Jonah had barely been in Nineveh one day when a remarkable spiritual awakening rocked the place. Jonah's message was short: "Yet forty days and Nineveh will be overthrown" (3:4). At that simple warning, Scripture tells us, "The people of Nineveh believed in God; and they called a fast and put on sackcloth from the greatest to the least of them" (v. 5). This pagan city repented of the evil they had done. The revival went through the entire population (estimated at about 600,000). Even the king "arose from his throne, laid aside his robe from him, covered himself with sackcloth, and sat on the ashes" (v. 6). It was the most extraordinary spiritual revival the world had ever seen. To this day history has never seen another awakening like what happened in Nineveh.

But Jonah was *not* pleased. His worst fear was coming to pass before his eyes. Still, he hoped to see God's judgment carried out. He camped on the east side of the city to see what would happen (4:5). What *did* happen is not as familiar to most people as Jonah's experience with the fish. But it reveals the main point of the Book of Jonah. God was giving Jonah a lesson about the glory of divine compassion.

These are the closing verses of Jonah. Jonah is bivouacked in the desert outside Nineveh, keeping his bitter vigil:

> So the Lord God appointed a plant and it grew up over Jonah to be a shade over his head to deliver him from his discomfort. And Jonah was extremely happy about the plant. But God appointed a worm when dawn came the next day, and it attacked the plant and it withered. And it came about when the sun came up that God appointed a scorching east wind, and the sun beat down on Jonah's head so that he became faint and begged with all his soul to die, saying, "Death is better to me than life."
>
> Then God said to Jonah, "Do you have good reason to be angry about the plant?" And he said, "I have good reason to be angry, even to death." Then the Lord said, "You had compassion on the plant for which you did not work, and which you did not cause to grow, which came up overnight and perished overnight. And should I not have compassion on Nineveh, the great city in which there are more than 120,000 persons who do not know the difference between their right and left hand, as well as many animals?" (Jonah 4:6–11).

That is surely one of the strangest finales in all Scripture. We are not told what became of Jonah. We have no idea whether his attitude changed after this, or if he remained the entire forty days, still hoping for the destruction of Nineveh. We get no glimpse of how Jonah responded in his heart to the Lord's tender admonition. We know nothing of his further ministry. History is even silent about the long-term effects of the revival in Nineveh. But the lesson God was teaching Jonah—and all Israel—was very clear. God is loving, merciful, patient, and compassionate toward sinners.

What happened to the prophecy of Nineveh's destruction? "When God saw their deeds, that they turned from their wicked way, then God relented concerning the calamity which He had declared He would bring upon them. And He did not do it" (3:10). Does this imply some changeableness in God? The *King James Version* is even more forceful: "God *repented* of the evil, that he had said that he would do unto them; and he did it not" (emphasis added). Is that not a contradiction of Numbers 23:19: "God is not a man, that He should lie, nor a son of man, that He should repent; has He said, and will He not do it? Or has He spoken, and will He not make it good?"

But this is no contradiction; it is an *anthropopathism*—a figure of speech that assigns human thoughts and emotions to God. Scripture uses anthropopathisms to explain to us truths about God that cannot be expressed in literal human terms.

Jonah 3:10 does not mean that God actually changed His mind. Quite the contrary; it was the Ninevites who changed. The turning away of God's wrath was perfectly consistent with His eternal loving character. Indeed, if He had *not* stayed His hand against Nineveh, *that* would have signaled a change in God, for this gracious promise overrides all His threatened judgments: "If that nation against which I have spoken turns from its evil, I will relent concerning the calamity I planned to bring on it" (Jer. 18:8).

The prophecy of doom against Nineveh was issued against a people who were haughty, violent, God-hating pagans. No such threat is ever uttered against humble penitents clothed in sackcloth and ashes. The revival utterly changed the people of Nineveh, so God stayed His hand of judgment and forgave them out of His love.

The God Who Loves

What happened was, of course, God's design from the beginning. Jonah seemed to understand this. He sensed that the prophetic warning was intended by God to turn the hearts of the Ninevites. That was why he fled toward Tarshish at the outset. Certainly God, far from being surprised by the turn of events, was sovereign over every detail of the unfolding drama. The One who oversees every sparrow—who even numbers the hairs on our heads—is supremely able to make all things work together for His own perfect ends. In every detail of everything, all His purposes are fulfilled and all His good pleasure is accomplished (Isa. 46:10). Nothing can thwart, frustrate, or improve the perfect plan of God. "Known unto God are all his works from the beginning of the world" (Acts 15:18, KJV). He providentially controls everything that comes to pass, according to a plan He decreed before the foundation of the world.

Throughout the Book of Jonah we see God at work in divine providence, sovereignly orchestrating all events in accordance with His eternal purposes. We are told, for example, that God appointed the fish that swallowed Jonah (1:17). Now in the closing chapter of the book, we read three times that God "appointed" certain things to be graphic illustrations to Jonah as God taught the prophet a lesson about divine compassion. These illustrations demonstrate how God determines even the smallest details of all that happens so that everything works together for His own glory and for the good of those who love Him. Here God was sovereignly directing everything, not only for the Ninevites' good, but for Jonah's good as well—even though what ensued was not entirely to Jonah's liking.

God gave the pouting prophet a series of object lessons to rebuke his lack of love for the people of Nineveh.

First, God *appointed a plant* to grow up over Jonah to shade Him from the desert sun during his vigil. Scripture says "Jonah was extremely happy about the plant" (4:6). Jonah probably saw the plant as a token of God's favor to Him. Perhaps he thought he could read the hand of divine providence in this event. After all, a single plant miraculously shooting up in the middle of the desert in just the right place to provide shade for Jonah *must* signify that God was on his side, not on the side of the Ninevites! Jonah might have even thought it meant God was preparing to destroy Nineveh after all. The prophet's mood immediately changed from anger to delight.

But at dawn of the very next day God *appointed a worm,* which attacked the plant so that it withered and died. Worse, God *appointed a hot wind* that sapped all the prophet's strength and suddenly made his circumstances thoroughly uncomfortable.

God was still working all things for Jonah's good, but the prophet did not see it that way. His mood changed again. Now he was angrier than ever. He even begged God to let Him die.

God rebuked the wayward prophet for his failure to understand divine compassion. He reminded Jonah that Nineveh was filled with young children ("more than 120,000 persons who do not know the difference between their right and left hand"). They would all be destroyed if God poured out His wrath on the city. The Lord pointed out that Jonah was so selfish about his own personal comfort that he had more feeling for the plant than for the people of Nineveh.

Notice how Jonah's irrational feelings for the plant ("for which you did not work, and which you did not cause to grow") contrast with God's compassion for His own creation: "Should I not have compassion on Nineveh, the great city . . . ?" Romans 9 echoes the same idea: "I will have mercy on whom I have mercy, and I will have compassion on whom I have compassion. . . . Does not the potter have a right over the clay?" (vv. 15, 21). If God chose to be merciful to the inhabitants of Nineveh, He had every right to display His saving love that way. On the other hand, Jonah—himself a recipient of God's wondrous grace—had *no* right to resent God's compassion for others. He also had no right to be so devoid of compassion toward these people.

The God Who Loves

From a human perspective, it is certainly understandable that Jonah, together with virtually all of Israel, would have preferred that God simply destroy Nineveh. But the human perspective is flawed. God is a God of patience, compassion, and grace. Because God was willing to show mercy to a wicked society, Jonah's preaching ushered in one of the most remarkable revivals in the history of mankind—in spite of Jonah himself. And God was glorified in such a display of His great love for sinners.

God's Gift of Repentance

GOD'S LOVINGKINDNESS and tender mercies lavished on such an evil culture give us insight into the very heart of God. It is His nature to love, to show mercy, and to have compassion. But mark this carefully: when He stayed His hand of judgment in Nineveh, He did not merely overlook the sins of that society and allow them to continue blithely in their pursuit of evil. He changed the hearts of the Ninevites. The revival was a miracle wrought by God. As Jonah himself testified, "Salvation is of the Lord" (2:9). God is the One who brought the Ninevites to repentance. He awakened them spiritually so that they mourned for their sins (3:8). They turned from their wicked way (3:10)—but it was God who turned them (Lam. 5:21, KJV: "Turn thou us unto thee, O Lord, and we shall be turned").

True repentance from sin is always a gift of God. Paul wrote Timothy a bit of advice that would have been apropos to Jonah: "The Lord's bond-servant must not be quarrelsome, but be kind to all, able to teach, patient when wronged, with gentleness correcting those who are in opposition, *if perhaps God may grant them repentance* leading to the knowledge of the truth" (2 Tim. 2:24–25).

The very act of the Ninevites' repentance was confirmation of the sovereign grace and loving mercy of God. Had He not turned their hearts, they would never have turned.

Yet they *did* turn, and almost immediately. "The people of Nineveh believed in God; and they called a fast and put on sackcloth from the greatest to the least of them" (3:5). The king shed his kingly garments, put on sackcloth, and proclaimed a fast. It was astonishing that a culture of wicked arrogance could be instantly reduced en masse to the lowest humility in sackcloth and ashes.

About this, Hugh Martin, a nineteenth-century preacher from Scotland, wrote,

> Doubtless, the hand of God is to be traced in this, and His power and gracious influence on their hearts. And a very wondrous work it is of the grace of God, that a city such as Nineveh—great, and violent, and proud, and of a haughty spirit—should have been so greatly, so suddenly humbled to believe the message of God. Surely God's Holy Spirit was with God's holy Word among them: and very powerful, though secret, were His operations. It is impossible to account for their faith without attributing it to the operation of God upon their hearts, and the sovereign mercy of God towards them. . . . When the Ninevites believed God, was this not a faith which was "not of themselves"? Was it not "the gift of God"?[5]

Some have suggested that the "faith" of the Ninevites stopped short of true, saving faith. But I do not share that view. It seems obvious from our Lord's own testimony that for multitudes in Nineveh this represented an authentic saving conversion. In fact, Jesus cited Nineveh's repentance as a witness against His own generation: "The men of Nineveh shall stand up with this generation at the judgment, and shall condemn it because they repented at the preaching of Jonah; and behold, something greater than Jonah is here" (Matt. 12:41; Lk. 11:32). An entire generation of Ninevites was thus brought into the kingdom of God solely by His loving grace.

What were the long-term effects of this revival? Neither Scripture nor history give us much information. What we know is not encouraging. Sadly, within a generation or so after this revival, Nineveh reverted to her old ways. As we shall see in the following chapter, God finally had to pour out His wrath on the city.

That brings to mind a crucial truth about God's love and goodness. "From everyone who has been given much shall much be required" (Lk. 12:48). God's grace and privileges are not to be taken lightly. With greater privilege comes greater responsibility. And those who sin against God's goodness only deepen their inevitable condemnation.

The history of Nineveh illustrates that truth in a graphic way. That one blessed generation saw the goodness of God when what they deserved was His wrath. Only eternity will reveal how many souls were swept into the kingdom in that glorious revival.

But the glory soon departed. The memory of the revival was short-lived. Tragically, the offspring of that revived generation of Ninevites returned to their forefathers' extreme wickedness. The mercy of God to that generation was soon forgotten. A younger generation returned to the sins of their fathers. God's goodness to the city of Ninevah became a distant memory. The revival was not even mentioned in any of the known records of Assyrian history. There is no evidence that the revival ever penetrated beyond Nineveh into the rest of the Assyrian nation. In fact, what we know of Assyrian history suggests that the revival's impact was limited to one generation and one city. Assyria as a whole remained hostile to the God of Israel. We would know nothing of how God's loving grace was poured out on the wicked city without the Old Testament Book of Jonah.

Those years after Jonah's revival were the very years when Assyria became the dominant world power, increasing in military might and political influence. Riding the crest of God's mercy, Nineveh became the most powerful city in the entire world—the nucleus of Assyrian domination. Meanwhile, Assyria continued to wage war against the people of God. Soon Jehovah God was once again more hated than feared by the Ninevites.

But God was not through with Nineveh. The final page of her history was not yet written. That wretched city, which had tasted so much of divine goodness only to spurn God Himself, was about to learn what a fearful thing it is to fall into the hands of the living God.

. . . *And the Severity of God*

He Is a God of Inflexible Justice

He Is a God of Irresistible Power

He Is a God of Infinite Mercy

He Is a God of Inconceivable Righteousness

Chapter 4

■

. . . And the Severity of God

M ORE THAN A HUNDRED YEARS passed from the time of Jonah until Nahum prophesied the final doom of Nineveh.

Nahum, like Jonah before him, was called specifically to prophesy against that city. The brief book that bears his name is his only known prophecy.

This time God's purpose was vengeance, not mercy. Jonah's message had brought a loving warning to the city. Nahum's message would be a pronouncement of doom. God was about to glorify Himself again, but now He would do it by displaying His *wrath* against Nineveh.

Shortly after Jonah's experience in Nineveh, the Assyrians—led by Sennacherib, whose palace was in Nineveh—stepped up their barbarous treatment of the Israelites. Assyrian rulers of this era were ruthless men who boasted of their own brutalities. They liked to torture their victims with slow, cruel means of death, and they were known for building monuments to their conquests out of mutilated human remains. Sennacherib was the worst of the lot.

Assyria was responsible for dragging the ten northern tribes of Israel off into captivity from which they never returned. The Assyrians under Sennacherib also came in military force against the southern kingdom during Hezekiah's reign. Through Nahum, God was in effect saying He would no longer tolerate the sins of such a nation or the persecution of His people. And since Nineveh was the capital city of Assyria, it was against the Ninevites that God pronounced His judgment.

Under Jonah's ministry—and despite Jonah's unsympathetic attitude—God displayed His love and compassion for the citizens of Nineveh. Now He would pour out His wrath. Either way, He received glory.

Nahum's prophecy gives us lucid insight into the character of God. Lest we behold His mercy and forget His severity, here is a reminder that ultimately a holy God must wreak vengeance against sin. God is a righteous Judge. For Him to fail to carry out judgment would be inconsistent with His glory, untrue to His Word, and a contradiction of who He is. In other words, the basis for His judgment is His own righteous character. His judgment is as essential to His glory as His love.

So in the most candid, vivid terms, Nahum sets forth the majestic character of God as Judge. Nahum's prophecy is noteworthy for its careful balance. The prophet outlines four aspects of God's judgment that show the perfect equilibrium of the divine attributes.

He Is a God of Inflexible Justice

JUSTICE IS A LEGAL term that describes the righteousness of divine government. God is a just God. His justice is as unchanging as any other aspect of His character. God cannot change His mind or lower His moral standards. Since He is utterly perfect, any change at all would diminish His perfection—and that would be unthinkable. So His justice is inflexible; His holy nature demands that it be so.

As Creator, He is entitled to rule over all His creatures any way He pleases. The Potter quite simply has power over the clay to fashion it any way He desires. He makes the laws; He determines the standards; and He judges accordingly. He created everything for His own pleasure; and He has every right to do so. He also has total power to determine the principles by which His creation must function. In short, He has the absolute right to do whatever He determines to do. And because He is righteous, He rules in perfect righteousness, always holding to the highest standard of truth and perfect virtue.

If any creature chafes under God's rule or rebels against divine government, that creature then falls immediately under the judgment of God. Anyone who does not conform to the will of God incurs the inflexible justice of God.

In other words, God's justice is *perfect* because He Himself is absolutely pure, utterly righteous, consummately just—He Himself is perfect. He cannot be unjust. That is precisely why His justice is inflexible.

Here is the description of God with which Nahum introduces his prophecy: "A jealous and avenging God is the Lord; the Lord is avenging and wrathful. The Lord takes vengeance on His adversaries, and He reserves wrath for His enemies. The Lord is slow to anger and great in power, and the Lord will by no means leave the guilty unpunished" (Nah. 1:2–3). Those are powerful statements, giving us an unmistakable look into God's character.

Notice it says God is "jealous." As a child, I was troubled the first time I heard that, because I pictured jealousy as an unwholesome trait. But this speaks of a righteous jealousy unique to God. He is intolerant of unbelief, rebellion, disloyalty, or infidelity. He resents the insults and the indignities of people who worship anything or anyone besides Him. He demands to be given His rightful place above all else that we love or worship.

Thus, someone might say, "God is self-centered."

But, of course; God alone has the *right* to be self-centered. In contrast to all His creatures, He is entitled to demand worship and be jealous of His own glory. He is God, and there is no one else like Him (Isa. 46:9). He, and He alone, has absolute authority to judge those who rebel against His laws, refuse to give Him glory, ridicule His authority, or doubt His Word. And He jealously guards His name against all who would diminish His glory. "I am the Lord, that is My name; I will not give My glory to another, nor My praise to graven images" (Isa. 42:8). *"For My own sake, for My own sake, I will act; for how can My name be profaned? And My glory I will not give to another"* (48:11, emphasis added). What would seem like unacceptable pride in any lesser being is the necessary expression of a holy God who refuses to have His holiness besmirched. God's jealousy is therefore a righteous jealousy.

This truth is taught in the first of the Ten Commandments: "I am the Lord your God, who brought you out of the land of Egypt, out of the house of slavery. You shall have no other gods before Me" (Exod. 20:2–3).

The second commandment forbids idolatry and explicitly describes God as jealous:

> You shall not make for yourself an idol, or any likeness of what is in heaven above or on the earth beneath or in the water under the earth. You shall not worship them or serve them; for I, the Lord your God, am a jealous God, visiting the iniquity of the fathers on the children, on the third and the fourth generations of those who hate Me (vv. 4–5).

The third commandment continues the same theme, warning those who would trifle even with the name of God: "You shall not take the name of the Lord your God in vain, for the Lord will not leave him unpunished who takes His name in vain" (v. 7). In Ezekiel 39:25 He echoes: "I shall be jealous for My holy name."

God's holy jealousy is so descriptive of who He is that He even takes the name "Jealous" as His own. "You shall not worship any other god, for the Lord, *whose name is Jealous,* is a jealous God" (Exod. 34:14, emphasis added).

And in Deuteronomy 4:24 we read, "The Lord your God is a consuming fire, a jealous God."

The message is clear: God is jealous for His glory, and to disgrace His honor in any way—by worshiping a false God, or disobeying the true God, or simply failing to love Him with all the heart, soul, mind, and strength—is to incite the jealousy of God and incur His holy wrath. Simply because of who He is, God is perfectly righteous to be jealous of His glory and to be angry at those who denigrate or defame Him in any way.

Ezekiel 38:18 is a graphic portrayal of God's righteous jealousy: "It shall come to pass at the same time when Gog shall come against the land of Israel, saith the Lord God, that my fury shall come up in my face" (KJV). There, in a classic anthropopathism, Scripture pictures God as so angry that His wrath wells up in His face—like someone who becomes red-faced with fury. Ezekiel's prophecy continues,

> "And in My zeal and in My blazing wrath I declare that on that day there will surely be a great earthquake in the land of Israel. And the fish of the sea, the birds of the heavens, the beasts of the field, all the creeping things that creep on the earth, and all the men who are on the face of the earth will shake at My presence; the mountains also will be thrown down, the steep pathways will collapse, and every wall will fall to the ground. And I shall call for a sword against him on all My mountains," declares the Lord God. "Every man's sword will be against his brother. And with pestilence and with blood I shall enter into judgment with him; and I shall rain on him, and on his troops, and on the many peoples who are with him, a torrential rain, with hailstones, fire, and brimstone. And I shall magnify Myself, sanctify Myself, and make Myself known in the sight of many nations; and they will know that I am the Lord" (vv. 19–23).

God tolerates no rivals; He permits no rebels. He is a jealous God.

And when the Lord Jesus Christ returns in glory, the wrath of God will be on display. Jude 14–15 tells us, "Behold, the Lord cometh with ten thousands of his saints, to execute judgment upon all, and to convince all that are ungodly among them of all their ungodly deeds which they have ungodly committed, and of all their hard speeches which ungodly sinners have spoken against him" (KJV).

So why all this attention to God's jealousy in a book that features His love? Quite simply because God's jealousy is an expression of His love. Jealousy is possible only in a love relationship.

God is jealous because He loves. He is jealous when those who are the object of His lovingkindness are drawn away by sin and evil to worship other gods. He is jealous when those who ought to love Him defy Him and set their love on lesser objects.

But the supreme jealousy of God is against those who spurn His beloved Son. Scripture says, "If anyone does not love the Lord, let him be accursed" (1 Cor. 16:22). Those who refuse love to the Lord Jesus Christ abide under God's curse—because He is jealous for His own Son. Thus God's love—particularly the Father's love for the Son—is inextricably linked to His holy jealousy. His love would actually be diminished if He relinquished His jealous anger.

Look again at Nahum's prophecy against Nineveh. Here we see that God's wrath—tempered by His great patience and lovingkindness for so many years—must inevitably give way to His avenging anger against sin. Notice the emphasis placed on divine vengeance in just the second verse of Nahum's prophecy: "A jealous and *avenging* God is the Lord; the Lord is avenging and wrathful. The Lord takes *vengeance* on His adversaries, and *He reserves wrath for His enemies*" (Nah. 1:2, emphasis added).

The repetition of this solemn concept gives the prophecy a tone that is both fearful and serious—and fittingly so. These are no idle threats. God is about to avenge His name against a wicked city that was once the recipient of His patience and compassion. Now Nineveh will find no mercy.

The concept of vengeance, like that of jealousy, often carries less than noble connotations. Jesus forbade us to have a vengeful spirit (Matt. 5:38–44). But again, God—precisely because He is God—has every right to unleash His vengeance against the wicked. In fact, He is righteous to do so. In Deuteronomy 32:35 He says, "Vengeance is Mine, and retribution." He has the exclusive right to judge evildoers, execute vengeance, and pour out His wrath against sin. Those are prerogatives of God and God alone.

In fact, the very reason *we* are not to seek our own vengeance is that judgment and condemnation are divine rights. Paul wrote the Romans, "Never take your own revenge, beloved, but leave room for the wrath of God, for it is written, 'Vengeance is Mine, I will repay,' says the Lord" (Rom. 12:19).

No one violates the glory and the honor of God, no one slights His Son, and no one attacks those He loves—then escapes His wrath. Nahum 1:3 simply says, "The Lord will by no means leave the guilty unpunished."

"The Lord . . . is furious" (v. 2, KJV). "Furious" is translated from two Hebrew words (*ba'al chemah*) that literally mean the Lord is "master of His anger." It speaks of a controlled fury—again, not a transient emotion, not a passion, but a fixed disposition. "God is angry with the wicked every day" (Ps. 7:11, KJV). His wrath is constant, unwavering—but it is a burning fury against all those who rebel against Him.

God's wrath is revealed from heaven against all unrighteousness and ungodliness of men (Rom. 1:18). His justice is inflexible, unbending, always consistent. He will reckon with all who rebel. He will take vengeance on all His adversaries, "He reserves wrath for His enemies" (Nah. 1:2) because it is just for Him to do so. "The Lord will by no means leave the guilty unpunished" (v. 3).

Sinners often presume on the mercy and goodness of God. He is slow to anger (v. 3)—patient, longsuffering, kind, and gracious. But no sinner should ever take the goodness of God for granted. No one should mistake His patience for weakness. No one should assume His kindness signifies permission to continue in sin and unbelief. No one should think of His love as an antidote to His wrath. His goodness is not given as a comfort for sinners, but for precisely the opposite reason: "Do you think lightly of the riches of His kindness and forbearance and patience, not knowing that *the kindness of God leads you to repentance?*" (Rom. 2:4, emphasis added).

Yet many *do* misinterpret God's goodness as apathy toward sin and a barrier to judgment. Second Peter 3:4 depicts this error taken to its extreme by mockers who in the last days will scoff at the threat of retribution: "Where is the promise of His coming? For ever since the fathers fell asleep, all continues just as it was from the beginning of creation."

No one should miss the real point of God's longsuffering. Though loving, He has no plan to overlook the transgressions of the wicked. "The Lord knows how . . . to keep the unrighteous under punishment for the day of judgment" (2 Pet. 2:9). He is not slack concerning His promises; just longsuffering (3:9).

Likewise, when Nahum writes, "The Lord is slow to anger" (1:3), he is warning his readers that they must not confuse God's patience with impotence. Look again at Nahum's words: "The Lord is slow to anger *and great in power*" (emphasis added). Those who believe they are safe from judgment because God has not yet poured out His wrath had better think again. His goodness is not weakness; and His forbearance is not indifference. "Vengeance is Mine, and retribution," says the Lord. "In due time their foot will slip; for the day of their calamity is near, and the impending things are hastening upon them" (Deut. 32:35). "The Lord will by no means leave the guilty unpunished" (Nah. 1:3).

Nahum's statement that God is "great in power" introduces the second of three aspects of divine judgment that he highlights.

He Is a God of Irresistible Power

NAHUM'S ENTIRE PROPHECY is a verbal display of the divine majesty and a paean to God's power. "In whirlwind and storm is His way, and clouds are the dust beneath His feet" (v. 3). Anyone familiar with the power of a cyclone understands the gist of this. Nahum is describing the majestic power of God's fury, and he uses three aspects of nature to make the point: God's power in the heavens, God's power over the waters, and God's power on the land.

In Psalm 19:1 David wrote, "The heavens are telling of the glory of God; and their expanse is declaring the work of His hands." The glory Nahum sees in the heavens is God's avenging power. God controls the whirlwinds, the storms, and the clouds (v. 3). Those natural wonders are not only displays of divine power, but also are frequently employed as instruments of His judgment. Clouds, for example, are often noted in Scripture as symbols of divine judgment. When Christ returns in judgment, He comes with the clouds and in the midst of great judgment, according to Mark 13:26 and Revelation 1:7.

In Nahum's prophecy not only the heavens, but also the waters represent God's vengeance. "He rebukes the sea" (Nah. 1:4). That, of course, reminds us of the dramatic account of Mark 4:39, when Jesus "rebuked the wind and said to the sea, 'Hush, be still.' And the wind died down and it became perfectly calm." Do you recall the disciples' reactions? "They became very much afraid and said to one another, "Who then is this, that even the wind and the sea obey Him?" (v. 41). They saw the awesome power of God in Christ, and they trembled before that power. They knew it was the power of a holy, omnipotent, avenging Judge. Perhaps their minds even went back to this verse in Nahum, and they remembered the prophecy of divine vengeance.

When Nahum wrote, "He rebukes the sea and makes it dry; He dries up all the rivers. Bashan and Carmel wither; the blossoms of Lebanon wither," he was foretelling the doom of Israel's enemies. Bashan, Carmel, and Lebanon were the boundaries of Israel. Of course, this prophecy had particular reference to Nineveh—a city well beyond Israel's borders, but home to an army that was threatening those very borders.

Nahum next spoke of God's power over the land: "Mountains quake because of Him, And the hills dissolve; Indeed the earth is upheaved by His presence, the world and all the inhabitants in it" (Nah. 1:5). Someday God—according to Revelation 6:12; 11:13; and 16:18–20—will shake the earth with an earthquake from which the world as we know it will never recover. Haggai 2:6–7 contains this prophecy: "For thus says the Lord of hosts, 'Once more in a little while, I am going to shake the heavens and the earth, the sea also and the dry land. And I will shake all the nations.'"

God controls the earth. He can shake it whenever He likes. The mountains quake at His presence (Isa. 64:3). The hills melt like hot wax before Him (Ps. 97:5). When He determines to shake the earth, He shakes it (Jdg. 5:5; Ezek. 38:20). His power is irresistible.

In Nahum 1:6, the prophet asks, "Who can stand before His indignation? Who can endure the burning of His anger?" The answer is that *no one* can stand before Him. This is a description of divine judgment: "His wrath is poured out like fire, And the rocks are broken up by Him."

Divine wrath did finally bring about the doom of Nineveh, and all Nahum's prophecies were dramatically fulfilled.

God's justice is absolutely inflexible. His power is absolutely irresistible. Our God is a consuming fire. No wonder the writer of Hebrews warns,

See to it that you do not refuse Him who is speaking. For if those did not escape when they refused him who warned them on earth, much less shall we escape who turn away from Him who warns from heaven. And His voice shook the earth then, but now He has promised, saying, "Yet once more I will shake not only the earth, but also the heaven." And this expression, "Yet once more," denotes the removing of those things which can be shaken, as of created things, in order that those things which cannot be shaken may remain. . . . For our God is a consuming fire (Heb. 12:25–29).

He Is a God of Infinite Mercy

BUT IN VERSE 7 Nahum introduces a brief interlude into his prophecy of doom against the enemies of Jehovah. He reminds the people of Israel, "The Lord is good, a stronghold in the day of trouble, and He knows those who take refuge in Him." The Hebrew word translated "take refuge in" conveys the idea of trusting, confiding in, and fleeing to for protection. It speaks of faith. Those who "take refuge in" the Lord are those who *believe in and trust* Him. In fact, the *King James Version* translates the verse like this: "The Lord is good, a strong hold in the day of trouble; and he knoweth them that trust in him" (emphasis added).

The Lord—the Judge Himself—is a stronghold for those who seek refuge in Him by faith. Those words in a nutshell contain the entire gospel of justification by faith. The same God who threatens judgment against the wicked lovingly, compassionately invites sinful souls in despair to find their refuge in Him. He alone will be their haven, their stronghold, their protection from divine judgment.

How does He shelter those who trust Him? He covers them with His own righteousness, which is theirs by faith (Phil. 3:9). That's why in the Old Testament He is called "the Lord our righteousness" (Jer. 23:6).

The Old Testament repeatedly reveals God as a shelter for believing Israel. Psalm 61 calls Him a refuge and a tower of strength, covering His people as a bird covers its chicks with its wings (vv. 3–4). In Psalm 140:7 the psalmist refers to the Lord as "the strength of my salvation, [who] hast covered my head in the day of battle." He is the rock, the fortress, the deliverer (2 Sam. 22:2). All that imagery has important implications for the doctrine of justification by faith. This theme in the Old Testament reaches its apex in Isaiah 53:11, where the prophet reveals that the Messiah, "the Righteous One, [God's] Servant, will justify the many, as He will bear their iniquities."

The fullness of the doctrine of justification is finally expounded in the New Testament, where the apostle Paul elucidates it most thoroughly in his epistles. There we learn that the very righteousness of God in Christ is imputed to believers— solely by faith and not owing to any works performed by the believing one (Rom. 4:4–6). Christ Himself has already fulfilled the righteous requirements of the law on behalf of believers, and died in their place to pay sin's dreadful price. All believers in Christ are therefore both freed from their guilt and vested with Christ's perfect righteousness. That is the only way guilty sinners can ever find peace with God (Rom. 5:1). This doctrine of justification by faith is the very heart and soul of genuine Christianity. No brand of faith that denies it deserves to be labeled Christianity.

The textbook definition of justification by faith is this: "Justification is a judicial act of God, in which He declares, on the basis of the righteousness of Jesus Christ, that all the claims of the law are satisfied with respect to the sinner."[1] In other words, God *declares* the believing sinner righteous because of Christ— not because of any actual righteousness on the part of the sinner himself. Some might suggest that Nahum 1:3 altogether rules out that sort of justification: "The Lord will by no means leave the guilty unpunished." The *King James Version* is even stronger: "[The Lord] will not at all acquit the wicked." A parallel passage makes the same point, with God Himself stating, "I will not acquit the guilty" (Exod. 23:7). "I will not justify the wicked" (KJV). If God will not justify sinners, we all seem to be in a hopeless state.

But this is precisely where the glorious light of New Testament revelation shines most brightly, revealing the true depth of God's love. He does not merely acquit sinners. He does not overlook their sin. In the Person of Jesus Christ, He made a once-for-all, infinite atonement for their sins. Now He covers them with His own perfect righteousness by imputing it to them through faith (Rom. 4:11). All genuine believers therefore stand completely justified before a righteous God. It is not a future hope but a present reality. It is not a drawn-out process, but an immediate divine act that occurs at the first moment of faith. God's holy wrath is appeased and His love is perfectly fulfilled in the salvation wrought by Christ. Thus, He Himself is truly the stronghold to which sinners may flee from His awful judgments.

Again we see that the love of God and His wrath are inextricably linked. It is impossible to study one without encountering the other. That is why Nahum places his accolade to the goodness and mercy of God in the midst of a passage about God's wrath. This verse is not a digression from his theme; it is at the heart of his message.

This juxtaposition of the wrath and goodness of God is frankly hard for many people to swallow. As we noted in chapter 1, liberal theology flatly denies that a God of wrath can also be loving. Those who hold the liberal view inevitably define God according to their own specifications. They imagine God as benign but impotent—unable to enforce His righteous standards or to stop evil things from happening. In other words, they deny that God is truly sovereign.

Others deny God's essential goodness. They see the effect of evil in the world—poverty, disease, human wretchedness, natural disasters, and other disorders—and they conclude that God is cruel or unloving—or even deny that He exists. They cannot envision that a sovereign being who is truly good would tolerate so much evil.

But Nahum knew God as both sovereign and good. There was no contradiction. The Lord is good; forty-one times in the Old Testament we are told that His mercy endures forever. Seven times we find the phrase, "The Lord is good." He alone is good (Matt. 19:17). His goodness is personified in Christ, the Good Shepherd (Jn. 10:11, 14). His universal goodness is revealed in all His works: "The Lord is good to all, and His mercies are over all His works" (Ps. 145:9). Psalm 33:5 says, "The earth is full of the lovingkindness of the Lord." All creation speaks of God's essential goodness.

Consider this simple thought: The Lord could have made everything brown! Brown grass, brown flowers, brown sky, brown sea. But He didn't. There is much for us to enjoy in the variety and the beauty of His creation. These things illustrate His essential goodness. God is good. His goodness is seen in all His works. Don't let the profundity of that truth escape you.

No one appreciates the goodness of God like those who seek their refuge in Him. They are the ones who know Him and love Him. They are the ones on whom He has set His eternal love. They have fled to Him as their stronghold, and found mercy. They experience His goodness like no others. They appreciate His love like no one else.

"And He knows those who take refuge in Him" (v. 7). Does that mean the only people He knows about are the ones who trust Him? Certainly not. Remember that the word "know" and its cognates are often used in Scripture as synonyms for love. "Cain knew his wife" (Gen. 4:17, KJV). The expression speaks of the most intimate kind of love—in this case, the sexual union between a man and his wife. When Scripture says God "knows" those who take refuge in Him, it means He loves them with the deepest, most tender, and most personal affection. It describes the intimacy of divine love, which is unparalleled by any earthly kind of love.

When Jesus said, "My sheep hear My voice, and I know them" (Jn. 10:27), He didn't mean He knows who they are. He meant that He has an intimate relationship with them. Similarly, when Jesus said, "I never knew you; depart from me, you who practice lawlessness" (Matt. 7:23)—He did not mean that He didn't know who those people were. He meant that He had never had the intimacy of a love relationship with them.

God intimately loves those who trust in Him. The knowledge of that love is the greatest of all delights that can be experienced by the human heart.

One of my favorite passages in all of Scripture is found in Micah 7:18–19:

> Who is a God like Thee, who pardons iniquity and passes over the rebellious act of the remnant of His possession? He does not retain His anger forever, because He delights in unchanging love. He will again have compassion on us; He will tread our iniquities under foot. Yes, Thou wilt cast all their sins into the depths of the sea.

That describes the infinite mercy of God displayed in the salvation of His people. If you have never personally known that love but your heart is stirred by the wonder of it, I urge you to turn to Christ in faith and seek refuge in Him.

He Is a God of Inconceivable Righteousness

IT IS TEMPTING TO CAMP on Nahum 1:7 and focus on the goodness of God. But we must note that it is only a one-verse interlude in a chapter that extols the utter righteousness of God in judging the wicked. The Book of Nahum, as we have noted, is a prophecy

73

of doom on a wicked city. Though the Ninevites of Jonah's day found in God a refuge from judgment, their descendants would bear the full brunt of God's wrath. Nahum 1:7 is a clear testimony that God is still good to those who seek refuge in Him, but the Ninevites of Nahum's day would ultimately provide an object lesson of a different sort: "Whatever you devise against the Lord, He will make a complete end of it. Distress will not rise up twice" (1:9).

God's judgment does not negate His essential goodness. Nor does His goodness alter the severity of judgment. God is longsuffering. But when He finally must act in judgment, He makes a complete end of it. Hardened sinners should take note and tremble.

Nahum's message in verses 10–14 foretells the defeat of the Assyrians. God's righteous contempt for their evil works is evident in His pronouncement against them:

> Like tangled thorns, and like those who are drunken with their drink, they are consumed as stubble completely withered. From you has gone forth one who plotted evil against the Lord, a wicked counselor. Thus says the Lord, "Though they are at full strength and likewise many, even so, they will be cut off and pass away. Though I have afflicted you, I will afflict you no longer. So now, I will break his yoke bar from upon you, and I will tear off your shackles." The Lord has issued a command concerning you: "Your name will no longer be perpetuated. I will cut off idol and image from the house of your gods. I will prepare your grave, for you are contemptible."

Like a field of tangled thorns, they were fit only for burning. Like drunkards, they were defenseless. And like dry stubble, they were powerless to withstand the consuming flames of divine wrath. The phrase, "one who plotted evil against the Lord, a wicked counselor," seems to refer to Sennacherib. Against the entire nation and all their idolatrous gods, the Lord prophesied total destruction.

The prophecy was fulfilled to the letter. We read in 2 Kings 19:35–37 that one night "the angel of the Lord went out, and struck 185,000 in the camp of the Assyrians; and when men rose early in the morning, behold, all of them were dead. So Sennachérib king of Assyria departed and returned home, and lived at Nineveh. And it came about as he was worshiping in the house of Nisroch his god, that Adrammelech and Sharezer killed him with the sword; and they escaped into the land of Ararat. And Esarhaddon his son became king in his place."

But that was only the beginning of the judgment of the Assyrians—and of Nineveh in particular.

Beginning in chapter 2, Nahum prophesies the destruction of Nineveh. Space and the limitations of our topic do not permit examination of his prophecy in detail, but note that it was fulfilled exactly as it is recorded. After a series of enemy attacks and natural disasters, Nineveh was overwhelmed by the armies of the Medes, and the city was utterly leveled. When Nineveh fell, the Assyrian Empire toppled along with it.

Twice in Nahum's prophecy the Lord tells Nineveh, "I am against you" (2:13; 3:5). About this, my late mentor, Dr. Charles L. Feinberg, wrote,

> Paul indicates (Ro. 8:31) that if God be for us, no one can successfully be against us. The reverse is true also: if God be against an individual or nation by virtue of sin, then no one can successfully be for that person or nation.
>
> When Assyria touched Israel, God said, "Behold, I am against thee!" This is inevitable if God is to be true to His promise to Abraham. He had solemnly promised that in just such instances He would curse those who had cursed the seed of Abraham. The truth of God's dictum is written in the fate of Nineveh.[2]

And so we see again that God's wrath is proof of His love. His judgment is linked to His faithfulness. And He is righteous when He judges.

Nineveh was finished as a city. To this day the site lies in ruins, giving mute testimony to the severity of God's wrath against sin.

But it is also a reminder of God's immeasurable love for His own people. The destruction of Nineveh freed Israel from centuries of grief at the hands of marauding Assyrians. It was God's message to a wayward nation that He still loved them.

God had chastened Israel severely for her sins. But His purpose in afflicting Israel was only corrective. Through Nahum, He assured them, "[The Assyrians] will be cut off and pass away. Though I have afflicted you, I will afflict you no longer" (1:12).

There is a vast and important difference between God's judgment and His discipline. Judgment is severe, final, destructive. Discipline is loving, tender, and corrective. "For those whom the Lord loves He disciplines, and He scourges every son whom He receives" (Heb. 12:6). His discipline has a loving purpose: "He disciplines us for our good, that we may share His holiness. All discipline for the moment seems not to be joyful, but sorrowful; yet to those who have been trained by it, afterwards it yields the peaceful fruit of righteousness" (Heb. 12:10–11).

His judgment against the wicked, however, is of a different character altogether. To the wanton unbeliever, "Our God is a consuming fire" (v. 29). "His calamity will come suddenly; Instantly he will be broken, and there will be no healing" (Prov. 6:15).

No one should be lulled into carelessness by the knowledge that God is loving and gracious. God's love is immeasurable, unfathomable, and inexhaustible. It is perfectly correct to say that God's love is infinite. But that does not mean His love negates His righteousness or overrules His holy wrath.

The Lord is good, and His mercy endures forever (Jer. 33:11). The countless redeemed throughout eternity will give testimony to that. "For the Lord will not abandon His people, nor will He forsake His inheritance" (Ps. 94:14). "But judgment shall return unto righteousness: and all the upright in heart shall follow it" (v. 15, KJV). Those who are not upright in heart—those who spurn God's love and follow their own ways—will ultimately suffer the same fate as Nineveh. That city, where the love of God was once poured out in so great abundance, finally perished in the fury of His wrath.

> Behold therefore the goodness and severity of God: on them which fell, severity; but toward thee, goodness, if thou continue in his goodness: otherwise thou also shalt be cut off (Rom. 11:22, KJV).

.

Everything I Need to Know
About the Love of God
I Learned in the Nursery?

Wrong Answers to the Hard Questions About God's Love

Wrong Questions Based on the Wrong Perspective of God

Wrong Inferences from a Faulty View of Divine Providence

Two Aspects of the Love of God

Chapter 5

Everything I Need to Know About the Love of God I Learned in the Nursery?

Jesus loves me, this I know,
For the Bible tells me so.

Fʀᴏᴍ ᴄʜɪʟᴅʜᴏᴏᴅ most of us have heard that God loves us. The Bible tells us that love is at the very heart of who God is: *"God is love"* (1 Jn. 4:8, 16, emphasis added) and He is "the God of love and peace" (2 Cor. 13:11). Those truths are so wonderful that they are always among the first things we teach our children about God. And that is as it should be.

But don't get the idea that God's love is only a child's subject. And don't think that you have mastered the subject by absorbing what you were taught as a child. This subject is certainly *not* child's play. As we have seen already, God's love raises some very complex and sometimes disturbing questions. These questions need to be thought through carefully and answered biblically.

I promised at the very beginning of this book that we would return to deal with some of the hard questions the truth of God's love brings to mind. Even after all we've learned about the issue in the preceding chapters, we must still admit that these questions are among the hardest dilemmas any pastor or theologian will ever be faced with: If God is love, why is the world such a theater of tragedy? If God is so loving, why does He allow His own people to suffer? If "God so loved the world"—then why does He allow all the suffering and torture and pain and sorrow and grief and death? If God is both loving and omnipotent, then why is the world such a mess? Why would a loving God ever allow wars and famines and disasters to cause so much human anguish?

If God is the loving Father of humanity, why doesn't He act like a human father who loves his children? Why does He allow His creatures to make choices that result in their destruction, when He could prevent it or overrule it? If God is a loving God, why did He allow sin in the first place, and why death?

There are more questions, and they get even harder: If God is love, why isn't everyone saved? Why are only *some* said to be "elect," chosen by God to eternal life (cf. Matt. 22:14; 2 Tim. 2:10)? Why would a loving God send people to hell to suffer forever? Why would a loving God devise a plan that has so many people going to hell for all eternity?

What kind of love is it that can control the world but allows the world to suffer the way it suffers? What kind of love is it that is sovereign and yet sends poor, suffering people to an eternal flame? How are we to understand that kind of love?

Wrong Answers to the Hard Questions About God's Love

THOSE QUESTIONS ARE REASONABLE, and they need to be faced honestly. It won't do to pretend such difficulties are easy to answer, or simply ignore them and hope they go away. Anyone who thinks deeply about God will eventually come face-to-face with those very questions and others like them. They are unsettling, vexing, even bewildering questions. Genuinely satisfying answers to them are elusive. There's no point in pretending such questions should pose no problems for the Christian.

In fact, history reveals that those who settle for easy answers to these questions often make shipwreck of the faith. Usually they will cite Scripture selectively and ignore half of some important biblical truth while grossly overemphasizing the other half. And so they tend to go to extremes. The casualty list of those who have run on the rocks over these questions is enough to make the discerning Christian realize that these are hazardous waters to navigate.

Universalism, for example, teaches that in the end everyone will be saved. Universalists believe that because God is love, He cannot eternally condemn anyone. In the end, they believe, hell will not even exist. Some teach that the devil and his fallen angels will be redeemed. As we shall shortly see, Scripture contradicts such a view (Rev. 20:10).

Another attempt to solve the dilemma posed by God's love is a theory known as *annihilationism.* Under this scheme, God takes believers to heaven and puts the rest out of existence. They experience no conscious punishment or suffering; they are judged by having their existence terminated. According to this view, therefore, there is no such place as eternal hell. Many cults and apostate denominations have embraced this doctrine.

A doctrine closely related to annihilationism is a theory known as *conditional immortality.* This view suggests that the human soul is transient until immortality is bestowed upon it. Since eternal life is given only to believers, all others simply pass into oblivion after the final judgment. This view is gaining popularity these days, but it too contradicts Scripture (Matt. 25:46; Rev. 14:11).

Those views may serve to salve human emotion to some degree, but they don't do justice to what Scripture teaches. Therefore, they are errors—and extremely dangerous ones at that, because they give people a false sense of safety. Jesus Himself described hell in graphic terms. In fact, He had more to say about hell than anyone else in Scripture. He described it as a place "where their worm does not die, and the fire is not quenched" (Mk. 9:48). He called hell "outer darkness; [where] there shall be weeping and gnashing of teeth" (Matt. 8:12; 25:30). He warned unbelievers about the judgment to come: "There will be weeping and gnashing of teeth there when you see Abraham and Isaac and Jacob and all the prophets in the kingdom of God, but yourselves being cast out" (Lk. 13:28). He described hell as "unquenchable fire" (Matt. 3:12) and a "furnace of fire" (Matt. 13:42). And He warned those who heard Him preach, "If your hand causes you to stumble, cut it off; it is better for you to enter life crippled, than having your two hands, to go into hell, into the unquenchable fire" (Mk. 9:43).

Furthermore, Revelation 14:11 describes hell's torments as unremitting and eternal: "The smoke of their torment goes up forever and ever; and they have no rest day and night." Revelation 20:10 states, "They will be tormented day and night forever and ever." Matthew 25:46 says, "These [unbelievers] will go away into eternal punishment, but the righteous into eternal life." That verse employs the same Greek word for "eternal" (aionios—meaning "perpetual, everlasting, forever") to describe both the bliss of heaven and the punishments of hell.

Embracing any of these theories also usually has the effect of making people indifferent to evangelism. They begin to feel comfortable that everyone will either be saved or put out of misery, so evangelism loses its urgency. The gospel seems less compelling. It becomes easy to kick back and think less about eternal matters. And that is precisely the effect these theories have had in churches and denominational groups where they have been espoused. As the churches become liberal, the "Christians" influenced by them become cold to spiritual things. Many times they deny the faith altogether. The history of universalism provides abundant evidence of this. Because the doctrine is at its heart a denial of Scripture, it is a sure road to serious apostasy.

But one can easily err in the other direction as well. As I noted earlier, there are some Christians who ponder the hard questions about divine love and conclude that God simply does not love people who aren't His own; He hates them. Under this scheme, there's no tension between the love of God and His wrath. There's no reason to wonder how God can love people whom He ultimately condemns, because you simply conclude that whoever He condemns He hates. The non-elect are people whom God never loved in any sense. People who hold this view are quick to remind that God is angry with the wicked (Ps. 7:11); that He loved Jacob but hated Esau (Rom 9:13); and that He hates those who practice wickedness (Prov. 6:16–19). They conclude that such hatred and genuine love are mutually exclusive. Therefore according to this view, the love of God is limited to the elect alone.

That view doesn't do justice to Scripture, either. It restricts God's love to a remnant, and pictures Him hating the vast majority of humanity. In terms of sheer numbers, it suggests that God's hatred for humanity overwhelms His love. That is not consistent with the God of Scripture, who is "compassionate and gracious, slow to anger, and abounding in lovingkindness and truth" (Exod. 34:6). It doesn't seem befitting for the One whom Scripture describes as "a God of forgiveness, gracious and compassionate, slow to anger, and abounding in lovingkindness" (Neh. 9:17). And it doesn't seem consistent with the truth of Psalm 145:8–9: "The Lord is gracious and merciful; slow to anger and great in lovingkindness. *The Lord is good to all, and His mercies are over all His works*" (emphasis added).

And what about "God so loved the world" (Jn. 3:16)? I realize that there are some good commentators who have tried to limit the meaning of the word "world" in this verse to the elect alone. As noted in chapter 1, however, that view seems to run contrary to the whole thrust of the passage. John Calvin correctly saw this verse as a statement that "the Father loves the human race."[1] In fact, the whole point of verse 17 is to assert that Christ's advent was a search-and-rescue mission, not a crusade for judgment: "For God did not send the Son into the world to judge the world, but that the world should be saved through Him" (v. 17). The point is that God's primary purpose in sending Christ was born out of love, not a design to condemn. Christ's purpose in coming was to save, not to destroy.

Inevitably, those who want to limit the meaning of "world" in verse 16 will suggest that "world" in verse 17 cannot include every individual in the world, unless this passage is teaching a form of universalism. The verse says Christ came so that the *world* might be saved through Him. Obviously not every individual in the world is saved. Therefore, they suggest, "world" in both verses must be limited to the elect alone, and the verse can only mean, "God so loved *the elect.*"

But "world" in this context seems clearly to speak of humanity in general. If we try to make the term mean either "every individual" or "the elect alone," the passage simply makes no sense. The word "world" here is a synonym for the human race. Humanity in general is the object of divine love. And verse 17 simply means that Christ came to redeem this fallen race—not every individual, but humanity as a race. Titus 3:4 also speaks of God's love in these very terms: "The kindness of God our Savior and His *love for mankind* appeared" (emphasis added). The whole sweep of these texts seems to be saying that in a broad sense God's love is set on the whole human race, not just the remnant of elect individuals.

Indeed, to make good sense of this passage, we must interpret the expression "world" in verses 16 and 17 as broadly as we understand the same word in verse 19: "And this is the judgment, that the light is come into the world, and men loved the darkness rather than the light; for their deeds were evil." Clearly the word "world" has a universal and corporate aspect that envelops more than just the elect alone. God's love is for the world in general, the human race, all humanity.

So how are we to understand Romans 9:13: "Jacob I loved, but Esau I hated"? Did God really hate Esau? Yes. He hated the evil Esau represented. He hated Esau's unbelief and sin and worldliness. And in a very real sense, God hated Esau himself. It was not a petty, spiteful, childish kind of hatred, but something far more dreadful. It was divine antipathy—a holy loathing directed at Esau personally. God abominated him as well as what he stood for.

Esau, for his part, hated the things of God. He despised His birthright and sold it for one bowl of lentil stew (Gen. 25:34). He brought nothing but grief to his parents (26:35). He plotted to kill his own brother (27:41). He married pagan women because he knew it displeased his father (28:8–9). He lived a careless, worldly life of utter disregard and disrespect for the God of his ancestors. Certainly God hated all that, as well as Esau himself.

It is worth pointing out that the passage Paul quotes in Romans 9 is Malachi 1:2–3. God was speaking of two nations, Israel and Edom, merely calling them by the names of their respective ancestors. The words "I have hated Esau" (Mal. 1:3) have a meaning that goes beyond Esau himself and encompasses the whole evil nation of Edom. The hatred this describes is not a petty, spiteful loathing, but a holy abhorrence of people who were thoroughly and absolutely debauched.

But God's hatred for Esau and the nation of Edom does not prove that He had no love, no compassion, and no charity whatsoever to Esau or his descendants. In fact, we know from Scripture that God was kind to this despicable nation. When the Israelites left Egypt on their way to Canaan, they passed through the land of Edom. God firmly instructed Moses, "Do not provoke them, for I will not give you any of their land, even as little as a footstep because I have given Mount Seir to Esau as a possession" (Deut. 2:5).

This holy hatred combined with lovingkindness implies no inconsistency or equivocation on God's part. Both love and wrath are reflections of His nature; He is loving, yet holy. He is compassionate, yet indignant over evil. As I have already noted, hatred and love are not necessarily mutually exclusive. Even in the range of human emotions, such feelings are quite common. Most people know very well what it is to hate and love the same object at the same time. One might, for example, have both sincere compassion yet deep revulsion toward a filthy tramp who has lived a life of dissipation.

Furthermore, as any parent knows, wrath and love do not rule out one another. We know that God is often angry with those who are the objects of His everlasting love. After all, before salvation, even the elect are enemies of God (Rom. 5:10); "children of wrath, even as others" (Eph. 2:3). Conversely, God genuinely and sincerely loves those who are the objects of His eternal wrath.

We simply cannot resolve the difficult questions about divine love by concluding that God actually withholds His lovingkindness, compassion, mercy, and goodwill from all but the elect.

So we must reject universalism, annihilationism, and conditional immortality. But we must also refuse the notion that God's hatred for the wicked rules out any love for them. How then shall we answer the hard questions about divine love?

One other solution is often suggested. It is to tell those inclined to ask hard questions, "Shut your mouth. You have no right to ask the question." People who take this approach will point to Romans 9:20–21, where the apostle Paul replied to a skeptic of God's sovereignty by saying, "On the contrary, who are you, O man, who answers back to God? The thing molded will not say to the molder, 'Why did you make me like this,' will it? Or does not the potter have a right over the clay, to make from the same lump one vessel for honorable use, and another for common use?"

Who are we to question God? That is what Paul asks. God is God. He will do whatever He wants to do because He is completely sovereign. He is the Potter. He decides what the pot will be like. And the pot has no right to object.

Obviously, that is all very true. God is God. We cannot comprehend His ways. Many of the questions we ask have answers we could never comprehend. Certainly we have no right to challenge God's motives. We are not entitled to subject Him to our interrogation, as if He were accountable to us. And sometimes the questions we raise do not even deserve to be answered. In the end, we will be left with many unanswered questions. That will bring us to Romans 9:20 and the inevitable place where we must simply close our mouths and stand in awe.

Before we get to that point, there are many things that we *do* need to understand. Romans 9:20 is a fitting response to a skeptic. It is appropriate for the person who will not be satisfied with knowing what God Himself has revealed. But for the truth-seeker sincerely wanting to understand God and His love, there is much in the Bible to help him come to grips with the hard questions before coming to a stop at Romans 9:20.

That is not to say that we can find all the answers to our hardest questions. We can't. Take, for example, the very difficult question of why a loving God does not redeem everyone. *If God is love, why does He send some people to an endless hell?* Why doesn't He redeem everyone?

We simply do not know. Scripture doesn't say. God Himself does not reveal to us the answers to those questions. Anyone who pretends to know more than God has told us is foolish.

Ultimately we reach the place where we must leave our questions to God and trust His essential righteousness, His lovingkindness, His tender mercy, and His justice. We learn to live with the *unanswered* questions in light of what we *know* to be true about God. At that point, Romans 9:20 becomes a satisfying answer, because we know we can trust the Potter. Meanwhile, as we search God's Word with an open heart, God's own self-revelation gives us a wonderful, marvelous, rich, comprehensible understanding of His love.

Wrong Questions Based on a Wrong Perspective of God

IN GRAPPLING WITH THE HARD QUESTIONS about God's love it is crucial to bear in mind that human tendency to see things from the wrong perspective. We cannot comprehend an infinite God with our finite minds. If we attempt to measure God from a human perspective, all our thinking about Him will be out of whack. And we sin against God when we think things of Him that are unbefitting of His glory.

God Himself rebukes those who underestimate Him by thinking of Him in human terms: "You thought that I was just like you; I will reprove you, and state the case in order before your eyes" (Ps. 50:21).

Remember how the book of Job ends? After all Job's suffering, and his friends' counsel that actually added to his sufferings, God rebuked not only Job's counselors, but also Job himself, for entertaining thoughts about God that were not sufficiently high. Both Job and his counselors were attempting to explain God in human terms. They were trying to make sense of what Job was going through, but their failure to see God as far above His creatures had skewed their view of what was happening. The counselors were giving the wrong answers, and Job was asking the wrong questions. God put some questions of His own to Job:

> Who is this that darkens counsel by words without knowledge? Now gird up your loins like a man, and I will ask you, and you instruct Me! Where were you when I laid the foundation of the earth? Tell Me, if you have understanding, who set its measurements, since you know? Or who stretched the line on it? On what were its bases sunk? Or who laid its cornerstone, when the morning stars sang together, and all the sons of God shouted for joy? Or who enclosed the sea with doors, when, bursting forth, it went out from the womb; when I made a cloud its garment, and thick darkness its swaddling band, and I placed boundaries on it, and I set a bolt and doors, and I said, "Thus far you shall come, but no farther; and here shall your proud waves stop"? Have you ever in your life commanded the morning,

and caused the dawn to know its place; that it might take hold of the ends of the earth, and the wicked be shaken out of it? (Job 38:2–13).

I love that portion of Scripture! God is recounting His own creative works, and asking if Job is wise enough to tell God how these things are to be done. From this point on, for three or four chapters, God lists the marvels of His creation and challenges Job to tell Him if he knows better than God how the universe ought to be run. Rather than seeking to vindicate Himself in Job's eyes, God simply appealed to His own sovereignty. "Will the faultfinder contend with the Almighty? Let him who reproves God answer it" (40:1).

Job, wise enough to know when he had said too much already, simply replied, "Behold, I am insignificant; what can I reply to Thee? I lay my hand on my mouth. Once I have spoken, and I will not answer; Even twice, and I will add no more" (vv. 4–5).

Then God asked Job, "Will you really annul My judgment? *Will you condemn Me that you may be justified?* Or do you have an arm like God, and can you thunder with a voice like His?" (Job 40:8–9). Job's questions, valid as they may have seemed for someone who had suffered all Job had suffered, actually cast aspersions on God's character. Job was stepping over the line if he thought he could justify himself at God's expense.

Job, by God's own testimony, was a blameless and upright man. There was no one like Job on the face of the earth (Job 1:8). Yet he suffered—probably more than anyone else had ever suffered. Job was not as deserving of such suffering as anyone else would have been. Why was he taking the brunt of so much catastrophe? Where was God's love and His sense of justice and fair play? It was inevitable that Job would struggle with some very difficult questions like those, as people do today.

But the moment his questions reflected misgivings about God—His wisdom, His love, His goodness, and the equity of His justice—Job and his friends had crossed the line. They were appraising God by human standards. They forgot that He is the Potter and we are merely the clay. So God rebuked them.

Job immediately saw his sin: "Therefore I have declared that which I did not understand, things too wonderful for me, which I did not know" (42:3).

We need to bear in mind as we ponder the love and the wrath of God that in many ways these things touch on knowledge "too wonderful" for us. "It is too high, [we] cannot attain to it" (Ps. 139:6). "Who has known the mind of the Lord, or who became His counselor?" (Rom. 11:34). "Who has directed the Spirit of the Lord, or as His counselor has informed Him? With whom did He consult and who gave Him understanding? And who taught Him in the path of justice and taught Him knowledge, and informed Him of the way of understanding?" (Isa. 40:13–14). And "Who has known the mind of the Lord, that he should instruct Him?" (1 Cor. 2:16). Those are the same kinds of questions with which God confronted Job.

Therefore as we ponder our own hard questions about God's love, we must take great care lest the very questions themselves provoke us to think inadequate or inappropriate thoughts about God or develop sinful attitudes toward His love and wisdom.

Wrong Inferences from a Faulty View of Divine Providence

WE DARE NOT make the error Job's counselors made, thinking we can observe the workings of providence and thereby discern the mind of God. Job's friends thought his sufferings were proof that Job was guilty of some secret sin. In reality, the opposite was true. Since it is clear from many scriptures that we cannot know God's mind, we must not try to read too much into His works of providence.

By that, I mean we cannot assume we know the meaning or purpose of every fortune or disaster that befalls. Often the unrighteous seem to prosper and experience God's goodness: "The tents of the destroyers prosper, and those who provoke God are secure, whom God brings into their power" (Job 12:6). "I have seen a violent, wicked man spreading himself like a luxuriant tree in its native soil" (Ps. 37:35). "Behold, these are the wicked; and always at ease, they have increased in wealth" (Ps. 73:12). So what often seems like divine blessing is no proof of God's favor. Don't think for a moment that prosperity is proof of divine approval. Those who think in those terms are prone to go astray.

On the other hand, the righteous frequently suffer: "Indeed, all who desire to live godly in Christ Jesus will be persecuted" (2 Tim. 3:12). "Unto you it is given in the behalf of Christ, not only to believe on him, but also to suffer for his sake" (Phil. 1:29). But God uses such suffering to accomplish much good: "God causes all things to work together for good to those who love God" (Rom. 8:28).

In other words, the very thing that seems good will end in evil for the impenitent and unbelieving. But for God's own children, even trouble and discipline are intended for good (Gen. 50:20). Therefore the greatest disaster from our perspective may actually be a token of God's lovingkindness.

The area where I live is active with earthquakes. Over the years we have experienced regular tremors. I never feel the earth shake that I don't also think of the infinite might of our God. At 4:31 A.M. on January 17, 1994, I was suddenly awakened by the most severe tremor I have ever felt. That earthquake, which lasted less than ninety seconds, leveled several freeway overpasses very close to my home. A high-rise medical office building in the vicinity dropped ten feet when the second floor collapsed. A large shopping mall was virtually destroyed. Hundreds of apartment buildings and homes were demolished. Sadly, several people asleep in one building were crushed to death when the ground floor crumbled underneath the weight of two upper stories. From a financial perspective it was the most costly natural disaster in the history of our nation.

Everyone seems to see the hand of God in such an event. In the midst of our city's crisis, we suddenly heard newscasters and civic officials openly discussing the awesome power of God and speculating on whether the earthquake (and a wave of other civic and natural disasters that had befallen southern California in recent years) might contain some message from the Almighty.

Someone noted that the epicenter of the earthquake was in an area well-known as a major production center for pornography. Sadly, many Christians were confidently declaring that the earthquake was God's judgment on the community. It was proof, they said, that God was finally fed up with the sins of southern California. This was such a topic of conversation that one of the major networks sent their top news anchor to interview me for a story on the earthquake as a judgment of God. One of the first questions the anchorman asked was whether I thought the earthquake was a divine judgment.

My response surprised him. I said I thought God had shown more mercy than judgment in the earthquake. After all, it occurred at an hour when most people were at home in bed, on a Monday that was a government holiday. Fewer people were on the roads than at any other time during the week. The national media had shown scenes of vehicles trapped on islands of roadway where portions of a bridge had collapsed in front of and behind them. Incredibly, not one vehicle had fallen to the ground below. Freeways collapsed, parking structures crumbled, and high-rise office buildings fell. Many people I know narrowly escaped death or serious injury. But of the millions of people living in the quake area, fewer than sixty were killed! In fact, the most remarkable thing of all about the earthquake was the low death toll.

On reflection, then, what most of the world saw as a catastrophe, what most Christians assumed was a severe judgment, was undoubtedly a token of divine mercy. It surely was a warning of greater judgment to come. But like most incidents that we deem tragedies, the quake undoubtedly held a mixture of both the goodness *and* the severity of God. In my estimation, the blessings far outweighed the calamity.

Clearly, however, we cannot know the mind of God. There are, therefore, many pitfalls to avoid in both asking and answering the hard questions about God's love. The subject is *not* child's play. With those things in mind, we can delve into what God Himself reveals in His Word—and surely we will find that it is a very fruitful study.

Two Aspects of the Love of God

IN THE CHAPTERS THAT FOLLOW, we're going to examine the love of God in even greater depth. We'll attempt to keep a balanced perspective of God's universal love for all men and women, and His particular love—a saving love—for His chosen ones, the elect. As we weave together many threads of thought, please try to avoid jumping to preliminary conclusions. Once we have a full picture of all that Scripture has to say about the love of God, all the different strands of truth will make a rich tapestry. Some things may not seem to make sense until we step back and look at the finished work. But when we see the big picture, it is breathtaking.

These two aspects of God's love—His universal love for all humanity, and His particular love for the elect—must not be confounded. To affirm that God loves the elect with a saving love is not to suggest that He has no love whatsoever for the rest of humanity. And to acknowledge that God genuinely loves even those whom He does not save is not to impute any kind of feebleness to God. In the end, none of His purposes are thwarted, and every aspect of His love perfectly declares His glory.

The Love of God for Humanity

Does God Love the Whole World?

Is God Sincere in the Gospel Offer?

Can God Really Love Those Whom He Does Not Save?

In What Sense Is God's Love Universal?

Chapter 6

The Love of God for Humanity

PERHAPS YOU HAVE NOTICED that someone shows up at almost every major American sporting event, in the center of the television camera's view, holding a sign that usually reads "John 3:16." At the World Series, the sign can normally be spotted right behind home plate. At the Super Bowl, someone holding the sign inevitably has seats between the goalposts. And in the NBA play-offs, the ubiquitous "John 3:16" banner can be seen somewhere in the front-row seats. How these people always manage to get prime seats is a mystery. But someone is always there, often wearing a multicolored wig to call attention to himself.

A couple of years ago, one of the men who had gained some degree of fame from holding up these "John 3:16" signs barricaded himself in a Los Angeles hotel and held police at bay until he was permitted to make a statement on television. It was a surrealistic image—here was someone who felt his mission in life was declaring John 3:16, and he was waving a gun and threatening police, while spouting biblical slogans. His career of attending major sporting events abruptly ended when police took him into custody without further incident.

As I watched the sordid episode unfold on television, I was

embarrassed that someone whom the public identified as a Christian would so degrade the gospel message. It occurred to me that I was watching someone whose approach to "evangelism" had never really been anything more than a quest for publicity. This stunt, it seemed, was nothing more than a large-scale attempt to get himself into the camera's eye once more. Sadly, he brought a horrible reproach on the very message he was seeking to publicize.

I also realized while watching that episode that John 3:16 may be the most familiar verse in all of Scripture, but it is surely one of the most abused and least understood. "God so loved the world"—waved like a banner at a football game—has become a favorite cheer for many people who presume on God's love and who do not love Him in return. The verse is often quoted as evidence that God loves everyone exactly the same and that He is infinitely merciful—as if the verse negated all the biblical warnings of condemnation for the wicked.

That is not the point of John 3:16. One has only to read verse 18 to see the balance of the truth: "He that believeth not is condemned already, because he hath not believed in the name of the only begotten Son of God" (KJV). Surely this is a truth that needs to be proclaimed to the world at least as urgently as the truth of John 3:16.

Does God Love the *Whole* World?

NEVERTHELESS, while acknowledging that some people are prone to abuse the notion of God's love, we cannot respond by minimizing what Scripture says about the extent of God's love. John 3:16 is a rich and crucial verse. In chapter 1, I noted that some Christians actually deny that God truly loves the whole world. I referred to Arthur Pink's famous attempt to argue that "world" in John 3:16 refers to *the world of believers* rather than *the world of the ungodly.*"[1] I pointed out that this notion seems to have gained popularity in recent years.

Perhaps it's worth revisiting this subject for a closer look. As I said, I am encountering more and more Christians who want to argue that the only correct interpretation of John 3:16 is one that actually limits God's love to the elect and eliminates any notion of divine love for mankind in general.

A friend of mine recently gave me seven or eight articles that have circulated in recent months on the Internet. All of them were written and posted in various computer forums by Christians. And all of them deny that God loves everyone. It is frankly surprising how pervasive this idea has become among evangelicals. Here are some excerpts taken from these articles:

☐ The popular idea that God loves everyone is simply not to be found in the Scripture.

☐ God does love many, and those whom He loves, He will save. What about the rest? They are loved not at all.

☐ *Sheer logic alone* dictates that God would save those whom He loves.

☐ If God loved everyone, everyone would be saved. It is as simple as that. Clearly, not everyone is saved. Therefore, God does not love everyone.

☐ Scripture tells us that the wicked are an abomination to God. God Himself speaks of hating Esau. *How can anyone who believes all of Scripture claim that God loves everyone?*

☐ God loves His chosen ones, but His attitude toward the non-elect is pure hatred.

☐ The concept that God loves all humanity is contrary to Scripture. God clearly does *not* love everyone.

❏ All who are not keeping the Ten Commandments of God can be certain that God does not love them.

❏ Not only does God not love everyone, there are multitudes of people whom He utterly loathes with an infinite hatred. Both Scripture and consistent logic force us to this conclusion.

But neither Scripture *nor* sound logic will support such bold assertions.

I want to state as clearly as possible that I am in no way opposed to logic. I realize there are those who demean logic as if it were somehow contrary to spiritual truth. I do not agree; in fact, to abandon logic is to become irrational, and true Christianity is not irrational. The only way we can understand any spiritual matter is by applying careful logic to the truth that is revealed in God's Word. Sometimes logical deductions are necessary to yield the full truth on matters Scripture does not spell out explicitly. (The doctrine of the Trinity, for example, is implicit in Scripture but is never stated explicitly. It is a truth that is deduced from Scripture by good and necessary consequence—and therefore it is as surely true as if it were stated explicitly and unambiguously.)[2] There is certainly nothing whatsoever wrong with sound logic grounded in the truth of Scripture; in fact, logic is essential to understanding.

But surely we ought to be wary lest "sheer logic alone" lead us to a conclusion that runs counter to the whole thrust and tenor of Scripture. Applying logic to an incomplete set of propositions about God has often yielded the bitter fruit of false doctrine. We must constantly check our logical conclusions against the more sure word of Scripture. In this case, the notion that God's love is reserved for the elect alone does not survive the light of Scripture.

As we have seen throughout this study, Scripture clearly says that God is love. "The Lord is good to all, and His mercies are over all His works" (Ps. 145:9). Christ even commands us to love our enemies, and the reason He gives is this: "In order that you may be sons of your Father who is in heaven; for He causes His sun to rise on the evil and the good, and sends rain on the righteous and the unrighteous" (Matt. 5:45). The clear implication is that in some sense God loves His enemies. He loves both "the evil and the good," both "the righteous and the unrighteous" in precisely the same sense we are commanded to love our enemies.

In fact, the second greatest commandment, "You shall love your neighbor as yourself" (Mk. 12:31; cf. Lev. 19:18) is a commandment for us to love *everyone*. We can be certain the scope of this commandment is universal, because Luke 10 records that a lawyer, "wishing to justify himself . . . said to Jesus, 'And who is my neighbor?'" (Lk. 10:29)—and Jesus answered with the Parable of the Good Samaritan. The point? Even Samaritans, a semi-pagan race who had utterly corrupted Jewish worship and whom the Jews generally detested as enemies of God, were neighbors whom they were commanded to love. In other words, the command to love one's "neighbor" applies to *everyone*. This love commanded here is clearly a universal, indiscriminate love.

Consider this: Jesus perfectly fulfilled the law in every respect (Matt. 5:17–18), including this command for universal love. His love for others was surely as far-reaching as His own application of the commandment in Luke 10. Therefore, we can be certain that He loved everyone. He *must* have loved *everyone* in order to fulfill the Law. After all, the apostle Paul wrote, "The whole Law is fulfilled in one word, in the statement, 'You shall love your neighbor as yourself'" (Gal. 5:14). He reiterates this theme in Romans 13:8: "He who loves his neighbor has fulfilled the law." Therefore, Jesus must have loved His "neighbor." And since He Himself defined "neighbor" in universal terms, we know that His love while on earth was universal.

Do we imagine that Jesus as perfect man loves those whom Jesus as God does not love? Would God command us to love in a way that He does not? Would God demand that our love be more far-reaching than His own? And did Christ, having loved all humanity during His earthly sojourn, then revert after His ascension to pure hatred for the non-elect? Such would be unthinkable; "Jesus Christ is the same yesterday and today, yes and forever" (Heb 13:8).

Look once again at the context of John 3:16. Those who approach this passage determined to suggest that it *limits* God's love miss the entire point. There is no delimiting language anywhere in the context. It has nothing to do with how God's love is distributed between the elect and the rest of the world. It is a statement about God's demeanor toward mankind in general. It is a declaration of *good* news, and its point is to say that Christ came into the world on a mission of salvation, not a mission of condemnation: "For God did not send the Son into the world to judge the world, but that the world should be saved through Him" (v. 17). To turn it around and make it an expression of divine hatred against those whom God does not intervene to save is to turn the passage on its head.

John Brown, the Scottish Reformed theologian known for his marvelous studies on the sayings of Christ, wrote,

> The love in which the economy of salvation originates, is love *to the world*. "God so loved the world, as to give His only begotten Son." The term "world," is here just equivalent to mankind. It seems to be used by our Lord with a reference to the very limited and exclusive views of the Jews. . . .

Some have supposed that the word "world" here, is descriptive, not of mankind generally, but of the whole of a particular class, that portion of mankind who, according to the Divine purpose of mercy, shall ultimately become partakers of the salvation of Christ. But this is to give the term a meaning altogether unwarranted by the usage of Scripture.[3]

B. B. Warfield takes a similar position:

Certainly here "the world" and "believers" do not seem to be quite equipollent terms: there seems, surely, something conveyed by the one which is not wholly taken up by the other. How, then, shall we say that "the world" means just "the world of believers," just those scattered through the world, who, being the elect of God, shall believe in His Son and so have eternal life? There is obviously much truth in this idea: and the main difficulty which it faces may, no doubt, be avoided by saying that what is taught is that God's love of the world is shown by His saving so great a multitude as He does save out of the world. The wicked world deserved at His hands only total destruction. But He saves out of it a multitude which no man can number, out of every nation, and of all tribes, and peoples and tongues. How much must, then, God love the world! This interpretation, beyond question, reproduces the fundamental meaning of the text.[4]

Warfield goes on to make the crucial point that our primary concern as we interpret the word "world" in John 3:16 should not be to limit the *extent* of God's love, as much as to magnify the rich *wonder* of it:

The key to the passage lies . . . you see, in the significance of the term "world." It is not here a term of extension so much as a term of intensity. Its primary connotation is ethical, and the point of its employment is not to suggest that it takes a great deal of love to embrace it all, but that the world is so bad that it takes a great kind of love to love it at all, and much more to love it as God has loved it when He gave His Son for it.[5]

In fact, as we noted in an earlier chapter, if the word "world" holds the same meaning throughout the immediate context, we see in verse 19 that it cannot refer to the "world of the elect" alone: "this is the condemnation, that light is come into the world, and men loved darkness rather than light, because their deeds were evil." About this, Robert L. Dabney wrote,

> A fair logical connection between verse 17 and verse 18 shows that "the world" of verse 17 is inclusive of "him that believeth" and "him that believeth not" of verse 18. . . . It is hard to see how, if [Christ's coming into the world] is in no sense a true manifestation of divine benevolence to that part of "the world" which "believeth not," their choosing to slight it is the just ground of a deeper condemnation, as is expressly stated in verse 19.[6]

So John 3:16 demands to be interpreted as speaking of God's love to sinful mankind in general. Calvin's interpretation is worth summarizing again here. You'll recall that he saw two main points in John 3:16: "Namely, that faith in Christ brings life to all, and that Christ brought life, because the Father loves the human race, and wishes that they should not perish."[7]

Now take a fresh look at John 3:16 and try to absorb the real sense of it: "God so loved *the world*," wicked though it was, and despite the fact that nothing in the world was worthy of His love. He nevertheless loved the world of humanity so much "that He gave His only begotten Son," the dearest sacrifice He could make, so "that *whoever believes in Him* should not perish, but have eternal life." The end result of God's love is therefore the gospel message—the free offer of life and mercy to anyone who believes. In other words, the gospel—an indiscriminate offer of divine mercy to everyone without exception—manifests God's compassionate love and unfeigned lovingkindness to all humanity.

And unless we mean to ascribe unrighteousness to God, we must affirm that the offer of mercy in the gospel is sincere and well-meant. Surely His pleas for the wicked to turn from their evil ways and live must in some sense reflect a sincere desire on God's part. As we shall see, however, there are some who deny that this is the case.

Is God Sincere in the Gospel Offer?

OF COURSE, PEOPLE who assert that God's love is exclusively for the elect will usually acknowledge that God nevertheless shows mercy, longsuffering, and benevolence to the unrighteous and unbelievers. But they will insist that this apparent benevolence has nothing whatsoever to do with love or any sort of sincere affection. According to them, God's acts of benevolence toward the non-elect have no other purpose than to increase their condemnation.

Such a view, it seems to me, imputes insincerity to God. It suggests that God's pleadings with the reprobate are artificial, and that His offers of mercy are mere pretense.

Often in Scripture, God makes statements that reflect a yearning for the wicked to repent. In Psalm 81:13 He says, "Oh that My people would listen to Me, that Israel would walk in My ways!" And, again, in Ezekiel 18:32 He says, "'I have no pleasure in the death of anyone who dies,' declares the Lord God. 'Therefore, repent and live.'"

Elsewhere, God freely and indiscriminately offers mercy to all who will come to Christ: "Come to Me, all who are weary and heavy-laden, and I will give you rest. Take My yoke upon you, and learn from Me, for I am gentle and humble in heart; and you shall find rest for your souls. For My yoke is easy, and My load is light" (Matt. 11:28–30). "And the Spirit and the bride say, 'Come.' And let the one who hears say, 'Come.' And let the one who is thirsty come; let the one who wishes [whosoever will—KJV] take the water of life without cost" (Rev. 22:17).

God Himself says, "Turn to Me, and be saved, all the ends of the earth; for I am God, and there is no other" (Isa. 45:22). And,

"Ho! Every one who thirsts, come to the waters; and you who have no money come, buy and eat. Come, buy wine and milk without money and without cost" (Isa. 55:1). "Let the wicked forsake his way, and the unrighteous man his thoughts; and let him return to the Lord, and He will have compassion on him; and to our God, for He will abundantly pardon" (v. 7).

There are some who flatly deny that such invitations constitute any sincere offer of mercy to the non-elect. As far as they are concerned, the very word *offer* smacks of Arminianism (a name for the doctrine that makes salvation hinge solely on a human decision). They deny that God would "offer" salvation to those whom He has not chosen. They deny that God's pleadings with the reprobate reflect any real desire on God's part to see the wicked turn from their sins. To them, suggesting that God could have such an unfulfilled "desire" is a direct attack on divine sovereignty. God is sovereign, they suggest, and He does whatever pleases Him. Whatever He desires, He does.

Let us be completely honest: this poses a difficulty. How can unfulfilled desire be compatible with a wholly sovereign God? For example, in Isaiah 46:10, God states, "My purpose will be established, and I will accomplish all My good pleasure." He is, after all, utterly sovereign. Is it not improper to suggest that any of His actual "desires" remain unfulfilled?

This issue was the source of an intense controversy among some Reformed and Presbyterian denominations about fifty years ago—sometimes referred to as the "free offer" controversy. One group denied that God loves the non-elect. They also denied the concept of common grace (God's non-saving goodness to mankind in general). And they denied that divine mercy and eternal life are offered indiscriminately to everyone who hears the gospel. The gospel offer is not free, they claimed, but is extended to the elect alone. That position is a form of hyper-Calvinism.

Scripture clearly proclaims God's absolute and utter sovereignty over all that happens. He declared the end of all things before time even began, so whatever comes to pass is in perfect accord with the divine plan.

What God has purposed, He will also do (Isa. 46:10–11; Num. 23:19). God is not at the mercy of contingencies. He is not subject to His creatures' choices. He "works all things after the counsel of His will" (Eph. 1:11). Nothing occurs but that which is in accord with His purposes (cf. Acts 4:28). Nothing can thwart God's design, and nothing can occur apart from His sovereign decree (Isa. 43:13; Ps. 33:11). He does all His good pleasure: "Whatever the Lord pleases, He does, in heaven and in earth, in the seas and in all deeps" (Ps. 135:6).

But that does not mean God derives pleasure from every aspect of what He has decreed. God explicitly says that He takes no pleasure in the death of the wicked (Ezek. 18:32; 33:11). He does not delight in evil (Isa. 65:12). He hates all expressions of wickedness and pride (Prov. 6:16–19). Since none of those things can occur apart from the decree of a sovereign God, we must conclude that there is a sense in which His *decrees* do not always reflect His *desires*; His *purposes* are not necessarily accomplished in accord with His *preferences*.

The language here is necessarily anthropopathic (ascribing human emotions to God). To speak of unfulfilled desires in the Godhead is to employ terms fit only for the human mind. Yet such expressions communicate some truth about God that cannot otherwise be expressed in human language. As noted in chapter 3, God's own Word uses anthropopathisms to convey truth about Him that cannot adequately be represented to us through any other means. To give but one example, consider Genesis 6:6: "The Lord was sorry that He had made man on the earth, and He was grieved in His heart." Yet we know that God does not change His mind (1 Sam. 15:29). He is immutable; "with [Him] there is no variation, or shifting shadow" (Jas. 1:17). So whatever Genesis 6:6 means, it cannot suggest any changeableness in God. The best we can do with such an anthropopathism is try to grasp the essence of the idea, then reject any implications we know would take us to ideas about God that are unbiblical.

That same principle applies when we are grappling with the question of God's expressed desire for the wicked to repent. If God's "desire" remains unfulfilled (and we know that in some cases, it does—Lk. 13:34), we cannot conclude that God is somehow less than sovereign. We know He is fully sovereign; we do not know why He does not turn the heart of every sinner to Himself. Nor should we speculate in this area. It remains a mystery the answer to which God has not seen fit to reveal. "The secret things belong to the Lord our God"; only "the things revealed belong to us" (Deut. 29:29). At some point, we must say with the psalmist, "Such knowledge is too wonderful for me; It is too high, I cannot attain to it" (Ps. 139:6).

Can God Really Love Whom He Does Not Save?

I REALIZE, OF COURSE, that most readers have no objection whatsoever to the idea that God's love is universal. Most of us were weaned on this notion, being taught as children to sing songs like, "Jesus loves the little children; all the children of the world." Many may never even have encountered anyone who denies that God's love is universal.

Yet if I seem to dwell on this issue, it is because I want to acknowledge that it poses a perplexing difficulty for other aspects of God's revealed truth. Let us honestly admit that on the face of it, the universal love of God is hard to reconcile with the doctrine of election.

Election is a biblical doctrine, affirmed with the utmost clarity from beginning to end in Scripture. The highest expression of divine love to sinful humanity is seen in the fact that God set His love on certain undeserving sinners and chose them for salvation before the foundation of the world. There is a proper sense in which God's love for His own is a unique, special, particular love determined to save them at all costs. (We will delve more deeply into this truth in forthcoming chapters.)

It is also true that when Scripture speaks of divine love, the focus is *usually* on God's eternal love toward the elect. God's love for mankind reaches fruition in the election of those whom He saves. And not every aspect of divine love is extended to all sinners without exception. Otherwise, all would be elect, and all would ultimately be saved. But Scripture clearly teaches that *many* will *not* be saved (Matt. 7:22–23). Can God sincerely love those whom He does not intervene to save?

British Baptist leader Erroll Hulse, dealing with this very question, has written,

> How can we say God loves all men when the psalms tell us He hates the worker of iniquity (Ps. 5:5)? How can we maintain that God loves all when Paul says that He bears the objects of His wrath, being fitted for destruction, with great patience (Rom. 9:22)? Even more how can we possibly accept that God loves all men without exception when we survey the acts of God's wrath in history? Think of the deluge which destroyed all but one family. Think of Sodom and Gomorrah. With so specific a chapter as Romans [1,] which declares that sodomy is a sign of reprobation, could we possibly maintain that God loved the population of the two cities destroyed by fire? How can we possibly reconcile God's love and His wrath? Would we deny the profundity of this problem?[8]

Yet Hulse realizes that if we take Scripture at face value, there is no escaping the conclusion that God's love extends even to sinners whom He ultimately will condemn. "The will of God is expressed in unmistakable terms," Hulse writes. "He has no pleasure in the destruction and punishment of the wicked (Ez. 18:32; 33:11)." Hulse also cites Matthew 23:37, where Jesus weeps over the city of Jerusalem, then says, "We are left in no doubt that the desire and will of God is for man's highest good, that is his eternal salvation through heeding the gospel of Christ."[9]

It is crucial that we accept the testimony of Scripture on this question, for as Hulse points out,

> We will not be disposed to invite wayward transgressors to Christ, or reason with them, or bring to them the overtures of the gospel, unless we are convinced that God is favorably disposed to them. Only if we are genuinely persuaded that He will have them to be saved are we likely to make the effort. If God does not love them it is hardly likely that we will make it our business to love them. Especially is this the case when there is so much that is repulsive in the ungodliness and sinfulness of Christ-rejecters.[10]

Biblically, we cannot escape the conclusion that God's benevolent, merciful love is unlimited in extent. He loves the *whole* world of humanity. This love extends to all people in all times. It is what Titus 3:4 refers to as "the kindness of God our Savior and His love for mankind." God's singular love for the elect quite simply does not rule out a universal love of sincere compassion—and a sincere desire on God's part to see every sinner turn to Christ.

Mark 10 relates a familiar story that illustrates God's love for the lost. It is the account of the rich young ruler who came to Jesus and began asking Him a great question: "Good Teacher, what shall I do to inherit eternal life?" Scripture tells us:

> And Jesus said to him, "Why do you call Me good? No one is good except God alone. You know the commandments, 'Do not murder, Do not commit adultery, Do not steal, Do not bear false witness, Do not defraud, Honor your father and mother'" (vv. 18–19).

Every aspect of Jesus' reply was designed to confront the young man's sin. Many people misunderstand the point of Jesus' initial question: "Why do you call Me good?" Our Lord was not denying His own sinlessness or deity. Plenty of verses of Scripture affirm that Jesus was indeed sinless—"holy, innocent, undefiled, separated from sinners and exalted above the heavens" (Heb. 7:26). He is therefore also God incarnate (Jn. 1:1). But Jesus' reply to this young man had a twofold purpose: first, to underscore His own deity, confronting the young man with the reality of who He was; and second, to gently chide a brash young man who clearly thought of *himself* as good.

To stress this second point, Jesus quoted a section of the Decalogue. Had the young man been genuinely honest with himself, he would have had to admit that he had not kept the law perfectly. But instead, he responded confidently, "Teacher, I have kept all these things from my youth up" (v. 20). This was unbelievable impertinence on the young man's part. It shows how little he understood of the demands of the law. Contrast his flippant response with how Peter reacted when he saw Christ for who He was. Peter fell on his face and said, "Depart from me, for I am a sinful man, O Lord!" (Lk. 5:8). This rich young ruler's response fell at the other end of the spectrum. He was not even willing to admit he had sinned.

So Jesus gave him a second test: "One thing you lack: go and sell all you possess, and give to the poor, and you shall have treasure in heaven; and come, follow Me" (Mk. 10:21).

Sadly, the young man declined. Here were two things he refused to do: he would not acknowledge his sin, and he would not bow to Christ's lordship. In other words, he shut himself off from the eternal life he seemed so earnestly to be seeking. As it turned out, there were things more important to him than eternal life, after all. His pride and his personal property took priority in his heart over the claims of Christ on his life. And so he turned away from the only true Source of the life he thought he was seeking.

That is the last we ever see of this man in the New Testament. As far as the biblical record is concerned, he remained in unbelief. But notice this significant phrase, tucked away in Mark 10:21: "Looking at him, Jesus felt a love for him." Here we are explicitly told that Jesus loved an overt, open, non-repentant, non-submissive Christ-rejector. He loved him.

That's not the only Scripture that speaks of God's love for those who turn away from Him. In Isaiah 63:7–9 the prophet describes God's demeanor toward the nation of Israel:

> I shall make mention of the lovingkindnesses of the Lord, the praises of the Lord, according to all that the Lord has granted us, and the great goodness toward the house of Israel, which He has granted them according to His compassion, and according to the multitude of His lovingkindnesses. For He said, "Surely, they are My people, Sons who will not deal falsely." So He became their Savior. In all their affliction He was afflicted, and the angel of His presence saved them; in His love and in His mercy He redeemed them; and He lifted them and carried them all the days of old.

Someone might say, Yes, but that talks about God's redemptive love for His elect alone. No, this speaks of a love that spread over the entire nation of Israel. God "became their Savior" in the sense that He redeemed the entire nation from Egypt. He suffered when they suffered. He sustained them "all the days of old." This speaks not of an eternal salvation, but of a temporal relationship with an earthly nation. How do we know? Look at verse 10: "But they rebelled and grieved His Holy Spirit; therefore, He turned Himself to become their enemy, He fought against them."

That is an amazing statement! Here we see God defined as the Savior, the lover, the redeemer of a people who make themselves His enemies. They rebel against Him. They grieve His Holy Spirit. They choose a life of sin.

Now notice verse 17: "Why, O Lord, dost Thou cause us to stray from Thy ways, and harden our heart from fearing Thee?" That speaks of God's judicial hardening of the disobedient nation. He actually hardened the hearts of those whom He loved and redeemed out of Egypt.

Isaiah 64:5 includes these shocking words: "Thou wast angry, for we sinned, we continued in them a long time; and shall we be saved?"

How can God be Savior to those who will not be saved? Yet these are clearly unconverted people. Look at verses 6–7, which begins with a familiar passage:

> For all of us have become like one who is unclean, and all our righteous deeds are like a filthy garment; and all of us wither like a leaf, and our iniquities, like the wind, take us away. And there is no one who calls on Thy name, who arouses himself to take hold of Thee; for Thou hast hidden Thy face from us, and hast delivered us into the power of our iniquities.

These are clearly unconverted, unbelieving people. In what sense can God call Himself their Savior?

Here is the sense of it: God revealed Himself as Savior. He manifested His love to the nation. "In all their affliction He was afflicted" (63:9). He poured out His goodness, and lovingkindness and mercy on the nation. And that divine forbearance and longsuffering should have moved them to repentance (Rom. 2:4). But instead they responded with unbelief, and their hearts were hardened.

Isaiah 65 takes it still further:

> I permitted Myself to be sought by those who did not ask for Me; I permitted Myself to be found by those who did not seek Me. I said, "Here am I, here am I," To a nation which did not call on My name. I have spread out My hands all day

long to a rebellious people, who walk in the way which is not good, following their own thoughts. (vv. 1–2)

In other words, God turned away from these rebellious people, consigned them to their own idolatry, and chose a people for Himself from among other nations.

Isaiah reveals the shocking blasphemy of those from whom God has turned away. They considered themselves holier than God (v. 5); they continually provoked Him to His face (v. 3), defiling themselves (v. 4) and scorning God for idols (v. 7). God judged them with the utmost severity, because their hostility to Him was great, and their rejection of Him was final.

Yet these were people on whom God had showered love and goodness! He even called Himself their Savior.

In a similar sense Jesus is called "Savior of the world" (Jn. 4:42; 1 Jn. 4:14). Paul wrote, "We have fixed our hope on the living God, who is the Savior of all men, especially of believers" (1 Tim. 4:10). The point is not that He actually saves the whole world (for that would be universalism, and Scripture clearly teaches that not all will be saved). The point is that He is the only Savior to whom anyone in the world can turn for forgiveness and eternal life—and therefore, all are urged to embrace Him as Savior. Jesus Christ is proffered to the world as Savior. In setting forth His own Son as Savior of the world, God displays the same kind of love to the whole world that was manifest in the Old Testament to the rebellious Israelites. It is a sincere, tender-hearted, compassionate love that offers mercy and forgiveness.

In What Sense Is God's Love Universal?

WHAT ASPECTS OF GOD'S LOVE and goodwill are seen even in His dealings with the reprobate? There are at least four ways God's love is manifest universally to all people.

The Love of God for Humanity

Common Grace

COMMON GRACE is a term theologians use to describe the goodness of God to all mankind universally. Common grace restrains sin and the effects of sin on the human race. Common grace is what keeps humanity from descending into the morass of evil that we would see if the full expression of our fallen nature were allowed to have free reign.

Scripture teaches that we are totally depraved—tainted with sin in every aspect of our being (Rom. 3:10–18). People who doubt this doctrine often ask, "How can people who are supposedly totally depraved enjoy beauty, have a sense of right and wrong, know the pangs of a wounded conscience, or produce great works of art and literature? Aren't these accomplishments of humanity proof that the human race is essentially good? Don't these things testify to the basic goodness of human nature?"

And the answer is no. Human nature is utterly corrupt. "There is none righteous, not even one" (Rom. 3:10). "The heart is more deceitful than all else and is desperately sick" (Jer. 17:9). Unregenerate men and women are "dead in . . . trespasses and sins" (Eph. 2:1). All people are by nature "foolish . . . disobedient, deceived, enslaved to various lusts and pleasures, spending [their lives] in malice" (Titus 3:3). This is true of all alike, "For all have sinned and fall short of the glory of God" (Rom. 3:23).

Common grace is all that restrains the full expression of human sinfulness. God has graciously given us a conscience, which enables us to know the difference between right and wrong, and to some degree places moral constraints on evil behavior (Rom. 2:15). He sovereignly maintains order in human society through government (Rom. 13:1–5). He enables us to admire beauty and goodness (Ps. 50:2). He imparts numerous advantages, blessings, and tokens of His kindness indiscriminately on both the evil and the good, the righteous and the unrighteous (Matt. 5:45). All of those things are the result of common grace, God's goodness to mankind in general.

Common grace *ought* to be enough to move sinners to repentance. The apostle Paul rebukes the unbeliever: "Do you think lightly of the riches of His kindness and forbearance and patience, not knowing that the kindness of God leads you to repentance?" (Rom. 2:4). Yet because of the depth of depravity in the human heart, all sinners spurn the goodness of God.

Common grace does not pardon sin or redeem sinners, but it is nevertheless a sincere token of God's goodwill to mankind in general. As the apostle Paul said, "In Him we live and move and exist . . . for we also are His offspring" (Acts 17:28). That takes in everyone on earth, not just those whom God adopts as sons. God deals with us all as His offspring, people made in His image. "The Lord is good to all, and His mercies are over all His works" (Ps. 145:9).

If you question the love and goodness of God to all, look again at the world in which we live. Someone might say, "There's a lot of sorrow in this world." The only reason the sorrow and tragedy stand out is because there is also much joy and gladness. The only reason we recognize the ugliness is that God has given us so much beauty. The only reason we feel the disappointment is that there is so much that satisfies.

When we understand that all of humanity is fallen and rebellious and unworthy of any blessing from God's hand, it helps give a better perspective. "Because of the Lord's great love we are not consumed, for His compassions never fail" (Lam. 3:22, NIV). And the only reason God ever gives us anything to laugh at, smile at, or enjoy is because He is a good and loving God. If He were not, we would be immediately consumed by His wrath.

Acts 14 contains a helpful description of common grace. Here Paul and Barnabas were ministering at Lystra, when Paul healed a lame man. The crowds saw it and someone began saying that Paul was Zeus and Barnabas was Hermes. The priest at the local temple of Zeus wanted to organize a sacrifice to Zeus. But when Paul and Barnabas heard about it, they said,

> Men, why are you doing these things? We are also men of the same nature as you, and preach the gospel to you in order that you should turn from these vain things to a living God, who made the heaven and the earth and the sea, and all that is in them. *And in the generations gone by He permitted all the nations to go their own ways; and yet He did not leave Himself without witness, in that He did good and gave you rains from heaven and fruitful seasons, satisfying your hearts with food and gladness* (vv. 15–17, emphasis added).

That is a fine description of common grace. While allowing sinners to "go their own ways," God nevertheless bestows on them temporal tokens of His goodness and lovingkindness. It is not saving grace. It has no redemptive effect. Nevertheless, it is a genuine and unfeigned manifestation of divine lovingkindness to all people.

Compassion

GOD'S LOVE to all humanity is a love of *compassion*. To say it another way, it is a love of pity. It is a broken-hearted love. He is "good, and ready to forgive, and abundant in lovingkindness to all who call upon [Him]" (Ps. 86:5). "To the Lord our God belong compassion and forgiveness, for we have rebelled against Him" (Dan. 9:9). He is "compassionate and gracious, slow to anger, and abounding in lovingkindness and truth" (Exod. 34:6). As we saw in an earlier chapter, "God is love" (1 Jn. 4:8, 16).

Again, we must understand that there is nothing in any sinner that compels God's love. He does not love us because we are lovable. He is not merciful to us because we in any way deserve

His mercy. We are despicable, vile sinners who if we are not saved by the grace of God will be thrown on the trash heap of eternity, which is hell. We have no intrinsic value, no intrinsic worth—there's nothing in us to love.

I recently overheard a radio talk-show psychologist attempting to give a caller an ego-boost: "God loves you for what you are. You *must* see yourself as someone special. After all, you are special to God."

But that misses the point entirely. God *does not* love us "for what we are." He loves us *in spite of what we are.* He does not love us because we are special. Rather, it is only His love and grace that give our lives any significance at all. That may seem like a doleful perspective to those raised in a culture where self-esteem is elevated to the supreme virtue. But it is, after all, precisely what Scripture teaches: "We have sinned like our fathers, we have committed iniquity, we have behaved wickedly" (Ps. 106:6). "All of us have become like one who is unclean, and all our righteous deeds are like a filthy garment; and all of us wither like a leaf, and our iniquities, like the wind, take us away" (Isa. 64:6).

God loves because He *is* love; love is essential to who He is. Rather than viewing His love as proof of something worthy in us, we ought to be humbled by it.

God's love for the reprobate is not the love of value; it is the love of pity for that which *could* have had value and has none. It is a love of compassion. It is a love of sorrow. It is a love of pathos. It is the same deep sense of compassion and pity we have when we see a scab-ridden derelict lying in the gutter. It is not a love that is incompatible with revulsion, but it is a genuine, well-meant, compassionate, sympathetic love nonetheless.

Frequently the Old Testament prophets describe the tears of God for the lost:

> Therefore my heart intones like a harp for Moab, and my
> inward feelings for Kir-hareseth. So it will come about when
> Moab presents himself, when he wearies himself upon his

high place, and comes to his sanctuary to pray, that he will not prevail. This is the word which the Lord spoke earlier concerning Moab (Isa. 16:11–13).

"And I shall make an end of Moab," declares the Lord, "the one who offers sacrifice on the high place and the one who burns incense to his gods. Therefore My heart wails for Moab like flutes; My heart also wails like flutes for the men of Kir-heres. Therefore they have lost the abundance it produced. For every head is bald and every beard cut short; there are gashes on all the hands and sackcloth on the loins" (Jer. 48:35–37).

Similarly, the New Testament gives us the picture of Christ, weeping over the city of Jerusalem: "O Jerusalem, Jerusalem, who kills the prophets and stones those who are sent to her! How often I wanted to gather your children together, the way a hen gathers her chicks under her wings, and you were unwilling" (Matt. 23:37). Luke 19:41–44 gives an even more detailed picture of Christ's sorrow over the city:

And when He approached, He saw the city and wept over it, saying, "If you had known in this day, even you, the things which make for peace! But now they have been hidden from your eyes. For the days shall come upon you when your enemies will throw up a bank before you, and surround you, and hem you in on every side, and will level you to the ground and your children within you, and they will not leave in you one stone upon another, because you did not recognize the time of your visitation."

Those are words of doom, yet they're spoken in great sorrow. It is genuine sorrow, borne out of the heart of a divine Savior who "wanted to gather [them] together, the way a hen gathers her chicks under her wings," but they were "unwilling."

Those who deny God's love for the reprobate usually suggest that what we see here is the human side of Jesus, not His divinity. They say that if this were an expression of sincere desire from an omnipotent God, He would surely intervene in their behalf and save them. Unfulfilled desire such as Jesus expresses here is simply incompatible with a sovereign God, they say.

But consider the problems with that view. Is Christ in His humanity more loving or more compassionate than God? Is tenderness perfected in the humanity of Christ, yet somehow lacking in His deity? When Christ speaks of gathering the people of Jerusalem as a hen gathers her chicks, is this not deity speaking, rather than humanity? Do not these pronouncements of doom necessarily proceed from His deity as well? And if the words are the words of deity, how can anyone assert that the accompanying sorrow is the product of Christ's human nature only, and not the divine? Do not our hearts tell us that if God is love—if His tender mercies are over all His works—then what we hear in Jesus' words must be an echo of the divine?

Admonition

GOD'S UNIVERSAL LOVE is revealed not only in common grace and His great compassion, but also in His admonition to repent. God is constantly warning the reprobate of their impending fate, and pleading with them to turn away from sin. Nothing demonstrates God's love more than the various warnings throughout the pages of Scripture, urging sinners to flee from the wrath to come.

Anyone who knows anything about Scripture knows it is filled with warnings about the judgment to come, warnings about hell, and warnings about the severity of divine punishment. If God really did *not* love the reprobate, nothing would compel Him to warn them. He would be perfectly just to punish them for their sin and unbelief with no admonition whatsoever. But He *does* love and He *does* care and He *does* warn.

God evidently loves sinners enough to warn them. Sometimes the warnings of Scripture bear the marks of divine wrath. They sound severe. They reflect God's hatred of sin. They warn of the irreversible condemnation that will befall sinners. They are unsettling, unpleasant, even terrifying.

But they are admonitions from a loving God who as we have seen weeps over the destruction of the wicked. They are necessary expressions from the heart of a compassionate Creator who takes no pleasure in the death of the wicked. They are further proof that God is love.

The Gospel Offer

FINALLY, WE SEE PROOF that God's love extends to all in *the gospel offer.* We saw earlier that the gospel invitation is an offer of divine mercy. Now consider the unlimited breadth of the offer. No one is excluded from the gospel invitation. Salvation in Christ is freely and indiscriminately offered to all.

Jesus told a parable in Matthew 22:2–14 about a king who was having a marriage celebration for his son. He sent his servants to invite the wedding guests. Scripture says simply, "they were unwilling to come" (v. 3). The king sent his servants again, saying, "Behold, I have prepared my dinner; my oxen and my fattened livestock are all butchered and everything is ready; come to the wedding feast" (v. 4). But even after that second invitation, the invited guests remained unwilling to come. In fact, Scripture says, "They paid no attention and went their way, one to his own farm, another to his business, and the rest seized his slaves and mistreated them and killed them" (vv. 5–6). This was outrageous, inexcusable behavior! And the king judged them severely for it.

Then Scripture says he told his servants, "The wedding is ready, but those who were invited were not worthy. Go therefore to the main highways, and as many as you find there, invite to the wedding feast" (v. 9). He opened the invitation to all comers. Jesus closes with this: "Many are called, but few are chosen" (v. 14).

The parable represents God's dealing with the nation of Israel. They were the invited guests. But they rejected the Messiah. They spurned Him and mistreated Him and crucified Him. They wouldn't come—as Jesus said to them, "You search the Scriptures, because you think that in them you have eternal life; and it is these that bear witness of Me; and *you are unwilling to come to Me,* that you may have life" (Jn. 5:39–40).

The gospel invites many to come who are unwilling to come. Many are called who are not chosen. The invitation to come is given indiscriminately to all. Whosoever will may come—the invitation is not issued to the elect alone.

God's love for mankind does not stop with a warning of the judgment to come. It also invites sinners to partake of divine mercy. It offers forgiveness and mercy. Jesus said, "Come to Me, all who are weary and heavy-laden, and I will give you rest. Take My yoke upon you, and learn from Me, for I am gentle and humble in heart; and you shall find rest for your souls" (Matt. 11:28–29). And Jesus said, "The one who comes to Me I will certainly not cast out" (Jn. 6:37).

It should be evident from these verses that the gospel is a *free offer* of Christ and His salvation to all who hear. Those who deny the free offer therefore alter the nature of the gospel itself. And those who deny that God's love extends to all humanity obscure some of the most blessed truth in all Scripture about God and His lovingkindness.

God's love extends to the whole world. It covers all humanity. We see it in common grace. We see it in His compassion. We see it in His admonitions to the lost. And we see it in the free offer of the gospel to all.

God *is* love, and His mercy is over all His works.

But that's not all there is to know about God's love. There is an even greater aspect of the love of God that is made manifest in His sovereign election and salvation of certain sinners. And it is to this higher kind of love that we now turn our attention.

The Love of God for His Elect

The Limits of Universal Love

The Magnitude of God's Saving Love

A Love That Is Sovereignly Bestowed

A Graphic Picture of Unfailing Love

God's Enduring Faithfulness

Chapter 7

The Love of God for His Elect

No ONE OUGHT TO CONCLUDE that because God's love is universally extended to all that God therefore loves everyone equally. The fact that God loves every man and woman does not mean that He loves all *alike*. Clearly, He does not. In Romans 9:13, the apostle Paul, quoting a prophecy from the Old Testament Book of Malachi, describes God's demeanor toward the twin sons of Isaac: "Jacob I loved, but Esau I hated."

Moreover, Paul says God made His choice when "the twins were not yet born, and had not done anything good or bad" (v. 11). Why? Why would God choose to love one and hate the other, before either of them could do anything to merit God's love or hatred?

Paul tells us why: "In order that God's purpose according to His choice might stand, not because of works, but because of Him who calls" (v. 11). Paul is teaching that God is sovereign in the exercise of His love. God has set His love on certain individuals in eternity past and *predestined* them to eternal life. Here, of course, we touch on the biblical doctrine of election.

Most people struggle with this doctrine when they first encounter it. Yet as we shall see, the doctrine is clearly taught in

Scripture. And it is so crucial to understanding the love of God that we must address it here.

The Limits of Universal Love

THE COMPASSIONATE LOVE and goodness God bestows on all humanity has its limits. It may be resisted. It may be rejected. It may be spurned. As we noted in the previous chapter, God's love and goodness *ought* to lead the sinner to repentance (Rom. 2:4), but because of the utter wickedness of the sinful heart, the sinner stubbornly persists in his sin and unbelief. Therefore, God's compassionate love and His goodness ultimately give way to hatred and judgment. The apostle Paul wrote in 1 Corinthians 16:22, "If any man love not the Lord Jesus Christ, let him be accursed." That is literally a pronouncement of damnation against those who spurn the love of God.

As we noted in an earlier chapter, some people would like to believe that God loves everyone so much that ultimately everyone will be saved. They suggest that even those who reject Him here on earth will be given a second chance on the other side of the grave— or that God will just summarily forgive everyone and take everyone to heaven. But Scripture holds forth no such hope. According to Jesus, the wicked are ushered into "eternal punishment" (Matt. 25:46). God's love spurned gives way to divine hatred, manifested in the animosity and vengeance of eternal judgment.

Others deny that God truly hates anyone. They will say that God hates the sin, but not the sinner. That is a false dichotomy, however. Remember that it is the sinner himself who is judged and condemned and punished. If God hated only the sin and not the sinner, He would strip the sin away and redeem the sinner, rather than casting the whole person into hell (Matt. 5:29; 10:28). Hell is, after all, the final expression of God's hatred. God does hate the reprobate sinner in a very real and terrifying sense.

I would never say such a thing were it not clearly taught in Scripture. Psalm 5:5-6 says, "The boastful shall not stand before Thine eyes; Thou dost hate all who do iniquity. Thou dost destroy those who speak falsehood; The Lord abhors the man of bloodshed and deceit." Psalm 11:5 says, "The Lord tests the righteous and the wicked, and the one who loves violence His soul hates."

The psalmist himself reflects the divine attitude when he writes, "Do I not hate those who hate Thee, O Lord? And do I not loathe those who rise up against Thee? I hate them with the utmost hatred; they have become my enemies" (Ps. 139:21–22).

As we have noted previously, this is not a malevolent hatred; it is a holy abhorrence for that which is vile, loathsome, and evil. But it is true hatred nonetheless.

So while there is a genuine sense in which God's love is universal in its extent, there is another sense in which it is limited in degree. The love of God for all humanity is not the sort of love that guarantees everyone's salvation. It is not a love that nullifies His holy abhorrence of sin. It is not a saving love.

The Magnitude of God's Saving Love

THERE IS AN EVEN GREATER LOVE of God, however, that does accomplish the salvation of sinners. It is a special love, bestowed from all eternity on those whom He has chosen as His own. God's love for those who believe—His love for the elect—is infinitely greater in degree than His love for humanity in general. Here we are talking about a very, very important doctrine of Scripture.

An entire chapter has already been devoted to demonstrating that God loves all humanity. For obvious reasons, that universal aspect of God's love is important to affirm. But it is even more crucial that we see that God has a special love for *His own,* His chosen people, and that He loves them with an eternal, unchanging love.

John 13:1 describes the love of Christ for His disciples: "Having loved His own who were in the world, He loved them to the end." Another version translates that same verse this way: "Having loved his own who were in the world, he now showed them the full extent of his love" (NIV).

That little phrase "to the end" (Jn. 13:1) is an important phrase. The Greek expression is *eis telos*. "To the end" is an acceptable translation, but idiomatically this is an expression that carries the meaning "completely, perfectly, fully, or comprehensively—to the uttermost."

God loves the world, but He loves "His own" perfectly, unchangingly, completely, fully, comprehensively—*eis telos*. Let me say it simply: He loves His own to the complete extent of His capacity to love His creatures. He loves them enough to make them joint-heirs with Christ. He loves them enough to make them into His very image. He lavishes them with all the riches of His grace for all of eternity. He loves them as fully and completely as any human could ever be loved by God—and His love knows no limits. That's what *eis telos* conveys.

This is also an unconditional love. Look at the context: Jesus was in the Upper Room with the disciples on the night He was betrayed. At this moment He was very much aware of their failures and weaknesses and their disappointing actions. They seemed to struggle to comprehend the simplest truths. They were a cowardly, disloyal, frightened group who would very soon scatter when He was taken prisoner. Christ knew this. He predicted that Peter would shamefully deny Him three times. He knew that when He hung on the cross the next day, most of the disciples would not even be present.

His love for them had never failed. He had proved it time and again. He even began their final evening together in the Upper Room by washing their feet, as if He were a lowly servant to them. Even after that, however, they interrupted the meal with an argument about which one of them was the greatest (Lk. 22:24)! He had loved them as magnanimously as was reasonable, and this is what He got in return.

To put it simply, His love for them was not repaid as it should have been. The disciples had ignored His love, taken it for granted, and abused it. But He loved them to the end. In other words, this was a love that would never die. It would never wane. It was *unconditional*.

But the expression *eis telos* also carries the idea of eternality. Here it speaks of a love that lasts forever. Not only did Christ love His own to the end of their lives; not only did He love them to the end of *His* earthly life; but He would love them eternally. In this same context, He tells them, "I go to prepare a place for you . . . that where I am, there you may be also" (Jn. 14:2–3). His love for His own will be manifest throughout eternity.

So the phrase *eis telos* is rich with meaning. "Having loved His own who were in the world, He loved them *[eis telos]*"—to the uttermost in every respect.

This, of course, speaks of the particular love of God for the elect. It is not the general love that extends to all humanity. It is not a conditional love that can give way to hatred. This is the love He has for "His own." It is a love that extends from eternity past to eternity future. And it is a love that will stop at nothing to redeem its object.

"Greater love has no one than this," Jesus said, "that one lay down his life for his friends" (Jn. 15:13). That is precisely what He would do for them the day after He spoke these words.

This love of God for His own is not bestowed on people because they show themselves worthy of it. In fact, there is *nothing* worthy in the recipients of this love:

> Christ died for the ungodly. For one will hardly die for a righteous man; though perhaps for the good man someone would dare even to die. But God demonstrates His own love toward us, in that while we were yet sinners, Christ died for us (Rom. 5:6–8).

The God Who Loves

These are not people who have somehow earned God's love. It is a wholly gracious love, not something anyone could ever earn through any kind of merit system.

Here is where the true greatness of divine love is seen. Christ faces the cross. He will bear their sin. And He will undergo the agonizing wrath of God on their behalf. He will suffer the painful, lonely sense of being forsaken by the Father, not to mention the human pain of execution and murder and public shame. And yet He is totally immersed in His love for His own, and as He faces death, He wants to affirm how much He loves these utterly unworthy men.

This is a love that only those who belong to Christ can possibly know. It is a unique and marvelous love. It is a life-giving love. It is a love that pursues its object, no matter what. It is a love that saves forever.

A Love That Is Sovereignly Bestowed

IN DEUTERONOMY 7:6, God told Israel, "You are a holy people to the Lord your God; the Lord your God has chosen you to be a people for His own possession out of all the peoples who are on the face of the earth." Here God is speaking about Israel, His chosen people. He says,

> The Lord did not set His love on you nor choose you because you were more in number than any of the peoples, for you were the fewest of all peoples, but because the Lord loved you and kept the oath which He swore to your forefathers, the Lord brought you out by a mighty hand, and redeemed you from the house of slavery, from the hand of Pharaoh king of Egypt (vv. 7–8).

God chose Israel not because they were better than the other nations, not because they were more worthy of His love, not because they were a greater or more impressive nation than any other, but simply because of His grace.

Someone might suggest that the words of Deuteronomy 7 are directed to an entire nation, including many who evidently were not numbered among the elect. After all, only a remnant from Israel was saved (Rom. 9:27–29). The apostle Paul, replying to a similar objection, wrote, "But it is not as though the word of God has failed. For they are not all Israel who are descended from Israel; neither are they all children because they are Abraham's descendants" (Rom. 9:6–7). In other words, election is not determined by blood descent. So taken in light of everything Scripture has to say about Israel, we know that the words of Deuteronomy 7 are actually addressed to the elect remnant.

Moreover, national Israel was only *representative* of all the elect of all time. God in His grace actually chose for Himself a people "from every nation and all tribes and peoples and tongues" (Rev. 7:9). When God speaks in Deuteronomy 7 of His eternal love for Israel, He is speaking of the spiritual children of Abraham. "Therefore, be sure that it is *those who are of faith* who are [true] sons of Abraham" (Gal. 3:7).

So the love God describes in Deuteronomy 7:6–7 is a particular love for the elect, and these verses therefore describe His love for *all* the elect. It is an eternal love, bestowed on the Israelites not because of anything worthwhile in them, but simply because it was the sovereign will of God to love them.

Why, of all nations, was Israel chosen as God's people? Because they chose God? No, because *God* chose *them*. That's exactly what Deuteronomy 7:7 means. It was God's sovereign choice to set His eternal love on Israel. In no way were they to think they were any more deserving than any other nation. It was a sovereign act of God's own will that He loved Israel. And out of His love, He chose.

The God Who Loves

A Graphic Picture of Unfailing Love

GOD HIMSELF, speaking through Ezekiel, explained His unique love for the elect in graphic terms. In Ezekiel 16, He pictures Israel in such loathsome and sordid terms that within Judaism itself this chapter is not permitted to be read in any public meeting. But this passage is not really about Israel's iniquity. It is about the eternality of God's love:

> Then the word of the Lord came to me saying, "Son of man, make known to Jerusalem her abominations, and say, 'Thus says the Lord God to Jerusalem, "Your origin and your birth are from the land of the Canaanite, your father was an Amorite and your mother a Hittite" (vv. 1–3).

Here God speaks to the city of Jerusalem, representing the Israelite nation. Jerusalem was God's own city, His dwelling place (Ps. 135:21). It was the center of Israel's life and worship. The temple was located there.

But something tragic had happened. Jerusalem was full of abominations. Idolatry was rampant. So the Lord instructed Ezekiel to make known to Jerusalem her own abominations. Ezekiel was to tell Israel that her father was an Amorite, and her mother was a Hittite (Amorite and Hittite being general names for the pagan dwellers of Canaan). The point was not literally that Israel descended from these tribes; they didn't. God was simply lamenting the fact that Jerusalem under Israel was no better off than when pagan tribes ruled Canaan. Israel had allowed things to regress to a state of paganism. They were acting like children of pagans rather than children of God.

In verses 44-45, Ezekiel repeats the same accusation, "Behold, everyone who quotes proverbs will quote this proverb concerning you, saying, 'Like mother, like daughter.' You are the daughter of your mother, who loathed her husband and children. You are

covenant. He treated her with the utmost tenderness, caring for her in her helplessness: "Then I bathed you with water, washed off your blood from you, and anointed you with oil" (v. 9). He bestowed on her all the favors that the wealthiest king might give his bride, lavishing her with the riches of His grace:

> "I also clothed you with embroidered cloth, and put sandals of porpoise skin on your feet; and I wrapped you with fine linen and covered you with silk. And I adorned you with ornaments, put bracelets on your hands, and a necklace around your neck. I also put a ring in your nostril, earrings in your ears, and a beautiful crown on your head. Thus you were adorned with gold and silver, and your dress was of fine linen, silk, and embroidered cloth. You ate fine flour, honey, and oil; so you were exceedingly beautiful and advanced to royalty" (vv. 10–13).

The love He showed Israel was extraordinary. This is what we would call today a "makeover" of major proportions. He turned this foundling riffraff into the most beautiful queen! In fact, this is precisely what God did when He brought Israel out of the slavery of Egypt to the brilliance and splendor of the Solomonic kingdom. Remember that the Queen of Sheba came just to see the glories of Solomon's kingdom (1 Ki. 10:1–13). All the beauty and magnificence of Israel at her height of glory were only because of the goodness of God.

But notice Ezekiel 16:15, "But you trusted in your beauty and played the harlot because of your fame, and you poured out your harlotries on every passer-by who might be willing." Israel became enamored with her beauty and greatness—and began having relationships with "every passerby who might be willing." That, of course, describes the spiritual harlotries of Israel, who after the reign of David repeatedly fell into sins such as worshiping idols and mixing pagan religious ideas with the worship God had commanded. Even Solomon himself "went after Ashtoreth the goddess of the Sidonians and after Milcom [Moloch] the detestable idol of the Ammonites" (1 Ki. 11:5).

God had chosen the nation in her helplessness, nurtured and cared for her until she was marriageable—and then wed her and adorned her with royalty. Now all of a sudden she was like a harlot on the street offering to commit adultery with any person who passed by. This is a disgusting, loathsome picture. But these are God's own words to Israel:

> "And you took some of your clothes, made for yourself high places of various colors, and played the harlot on them, which should never come about nor happen. You also took your beautiful jewels made of My gold and of My silver, which I had given you, and made for yourself male images that you might play the harlot with them. Then you took your embroidered cloth and covered them, and offered My oil and My incense before them. Also My bread which I gave you, fine flour, oil, and honey with which I fed you, you would offer before them for a soothing aroma; so it happened," declares the Lord God (Ezek. 16:16–19).

Israel took the very advantages God had graciously granted her, and turned those blessings into the instruments of her spiritual adulteries. She used God's gifts and His blessings in her own acts of unfaithfulness. She used the riches He gave to buy idols. She used her national stature to make alliances with pagan nations. The Israelites took the abundant goodness they derived from that land that flowed with milk and honey—and they offered it to foreign gods.

Worst of all, they engaged in the grossest kind of godlessness:

> "Moreover, you took your sons and daughters whom you had borne to Me, and you sacrificed them to idols to be devoured. Were your harlotries so small a matter? You

slaughtered My children, and offered them up to idols by causing them to pass through the fire" (vv. 20–21).

In other words, they took their own babies—helpless infants just as Israel was when God found her—and they put them on a fire to appease Moloch, the horrible god of the Ammonites. It was the Ammonites' practice to sacrifice their own children to Moloch by placing the infants on an open fire and roasting them alive (Lev. 20:2–5). This was one of the very reasons the Lord had ordered the Israelites to utterly destroy the inhabitants of the land before them (Lev. 18:21, 24–26).

On top of all this, Israel forgot the grace of God: "And besides all your abominations and harlotries you did not remember the days of your youth, when you were naked and bare and squirming in your blood" (Ezek. 16:22). She had returned the land to the sins of its pagan inhabitants. And as the Lord Himself said, "Yet you have not merely walked in their ways or done according to their abominations; but, as if that were too little, you acted more corruptly in all your conduct than they" (v. 47). Verse 27 says the sins of Israel were enough to shame even the Philistines!

Israel had made her own God a laughingstock among the nations. Try to dream up the grossest, most heinous imaginable kind of idolatry, and it would not outdo what Israel had done. It was as if they had gone out of the way to make their sins as public and as shameful as they could. They then sought more ways to indulge in idolatry:

> "Then it came about after all your wickedness, 'Woe, woe to you!' declares the Lord God), that you built yourself a shrine and made yourself a high place in every square. You built yourself a high place at the top of every street, and made your beauty abominable; and you spread your legs to every passer-by to multiply your harlotry" (vv. 23-25).

God continues to recount how Israel sought to commit her spiritual adulteries with the Egyptians (v. 26), the Assyrians (v. 28), and the Chaldeans (v. 29). "How languishing is your heart," declares the Lord God, "while you do all these things, the actions of a bold-faced harlot" (v. 30).

But this was even *worse* than harlotry! A harlot was paid for her favors God said to Israel, "In disdaining money, you were not like a harlot" (v. 31). Israel was willing to commit wanton adultery shamelessly, and for nothing in return. They weren't "selling out"; they were being unfaithful to God out of sheer lust for idolatry! Worse still—

> "You adulteress wife, who takes strangers instead of her husband! Men give gifts to all harlots, but *you give your gifts to all your lovers to bribe them to come to you* from every direction for your harlotries. Thus you are different from those women in your harlotries, in that *no one plays the harlot as you do, because you give money and no money is given you;* thus you are different" (vv. 32–33, emphasis added).

Israel was like a woman so lustful, she was paying for illicit lovers.

Do you see the degree to which Israel had gone in sinning against the Lord? Her lust for idolatry was insatiable. She had sinned against God in every conceivable fashion—and was still thirsting for more ways of committing her spiritual adulteries.

And so in verses 35–59, God pronounced a stern judgment on Israel. Her own lovers would abuse her:

> "I shall also give you into the hands of your lovers, and they will tear down your shrines, demolish your high places, strip you of your clothing, take away your jewels, and will leave you naked and bare. They will incite a crowd against you, and they will stone you and cut you to pieces with their swords" (vv. 39–40).

Israel had been haughty in her sinning. She had dishonored God and profaned His name before all the nations. Now God would dishonor her openly as well:

> "So I shall calm My fury against you, and My jealousy will depart from you, and I shall be pacified and angry no more. Because you have not remembered the days of your youth but have enraged Me by all these things, behold, I in turn will bring your conduct down on your own head," declares the Lord God, "so that you will not commit this lewdness on top of all your other abominations" (vv. 42–43).

This was a prophecy foretelling the Babylonian captivity. Israel was defeated by the Babylonians. Her cities and towns were plundered and burned. Her sons and daughters were taken captive into a foreign land. Her sin bore the inevitable fruit of shame and degradation and ultimate earthly disgrace. Having "despised the oath by breaking the covenant" (v. 59), Israel returned herself to a worse state than when the Lord originally found her.

But here is the astonishing part—though it may appear to the observer as if God had cast off His own people at this point, His love for Israel still moved Him:

> "Nevertheless, I will remember My covenant with you in the days of your youth, and I will establish an everlasting covenant with you. Then you will remember your ways and be ashamed when you receive your sisters, both your older and your younger; and I will give them to you as daughters, but not because of your covenant "(vv. 60–61).

Note that God did *not* say, "I will hate you with a holy hatred." Why? Why did He not treat Israel as He had treated the Sodomites, if as He said in verse 48, Israel's sins were worse than Sodom's? And why did He not forgive Samaria for their sins, if as the Lord Himself said in verse 51, "Samaria did not commit half of [Israel's] sins"?

It was simply and only because God had set His eternal love on Israel. These were the people whom He had chosen to love and with whom He had made an everlasting covenant. He loved them as fully as He had a capacity to love. Since in the first place His love was not because of anything *worthy* He found in the Israelites, nothing *unworthy* in them could destroy His love. His love for them was eternal and unconditional. Therefore it was a love rooted in God Himself. This is the particular love of God for His elect.

Notice, now, the conclusion of this chapter in verses 62–63:

> "Thus I will establish My covenant with you, and you shall know that I am the Lord, in order that you may remember and be ashamed, and never open your mouth anymore because of your humiliation, when I have forgiven you for all that you have done," the Lord God declares.

God silenced Israel. He reduced her to humiliation. How? By forgiving her. He accomplished it with His love.

Why didn't God forgive Sodom? They weren't His elect. Why didn't He forgive Samaria? He never made a covenant with them.

God loves whom He chooses to love. He makes a covenant with those people, and that covenant is an everlasting covenant made in eternity past. It guarantees redemption for the objects of God's particular love. Sodom was destroyed and unredeemed. Samaria was likewise condemned. But Israel, whose sins were worse than both, God forgave.

God's Enduring Faithfulness

WHY IS IT that God would so forgive Israel? Because He set His love on her *and made Israel His own possession.* They were *His own* in a unique sense—the same sense in which Jesus says of all the elect, "I am the good shepherd; and I know My own, and My own know Me" (Jn. 10:14). His love for His own is a far greater degree of love than the compassionate love He has for the whole world. This love is perfect. This love is comprehensive. This love is complete. This love is redemptive. This love is eternal. It is this love that caused Him to lay down His life for His own (Jn. 10:15).

The example we've looked at in Ezekiel 16 applies this special love of God in a national sense. Remember, however, that "For they are not all Israel who are descended from Israel" (Rom. 9:6). God's election of Israel was not a blanket choosing of every individual in the nation. But as the apostle Paul says, the promise is confirmed only to "those who are of the faith of Abraham."

Yet there is nevertheless a sense in which the *nation* of Israel was chosen by God above every other earthly race or tribe or tongue. "They were entrusted with the oracles of God" (Rom. 3:2). So, we might legitimately ask, "If some did not believe, [does] their unbelief . . . nullify the faithfulness of God?" (v. 3). If Israel is elect, how is it that the vast majority of Jews now reject their own Messiah? "God has not rejected His people, has He?" (Rom. 11:1). Paul spends three chapters addressing this very issue (Rom. 9–11), just after he expounds the great truth that God's love for His elect is inviolable (Rom. 8:35–39). Paul's answer: Israel's current unbelief does not nullify the faithfulness of God. God for His own purposes is currently "taking from among the Gentiles a people for His name" (Acts 15:14). But His love for Israel is undiminished.

In the first place, Paul says, there is "at the present time a remnant according to God's gracious choice" (Rom. 11:5). God still graciously calls a faithful remnant from among Israel. There are many, many Jews who do recognize Jesus as the true Messiah.

But in the second place, Paul tells us, there is coming a day when "all Israel will be saved; just as it is written, 'The Deliverer will come from Zion, He will remove ungodliness from Jacob'" (v. 26). In the greatest revival the world has ever seen, God will one day turn the entire Jewish nation to faith in their true Messiah. As Isaiah wrote, "Israel shall be saved in the Lord with an everlasting salvation: ye shall not be ashamed nor confounded world without end" (Isa. 45:17, KJV). Speaking of that glorious day, Jeremiah adds, "At that time they shall call Jerusalem 'The Throne of the Lord,' and all the nations will be gathered to it, to Jerusalem, for the name of the Lord; nor shall they walk anymore after the stubbornness of their evil heart. In those days the house of Judah will walk with the house of Israel, and they will come together from the land of the north to the land that I gave your fathers as an inheritance" (Jer. 3:17–18).

How can we be certain that God will do this? "This is My covenant with them, when I take away their sins" (Rom. 11:27). He has eternally covenanted to do it, and "the gifts and the calling of God are irrevocable" (v. 29). Therefore, "God has not rejected His people whom He foreknew" (v. 2). The current apostasy of Israel does not invalidate the eternality of God's love.

Bear in mind also that God's electing love is individual as well as corporate. Those whom God has elected are *individuals*. Even the election of Israel involves the choosing of a remnant of individuals. Within the nation, God deals with people individually: "That which Israel is seeking for, it has not obtained, but *those who were chosen obtained it,* and the rest were hardened" (Rom. 11:7, emphasis added).

A powerful example of this is found in the Old Testament account of the sordid tale of David's adultery with Bathsheba. Remember that David lusted after Bathsheba, committed adultery with her, impregnated her, then had her husband killed to try to cover the sin. Bathsheba became David's wife, but David did not repent of his sin until after the birth of the child. Moreover, the child conceived in that act of adultery died soon after birth. Scripture describes David's horrible agony over the death of his son, made all the more bitter by his shame for his own sin. Bathsheba, we assume, was equally distraught.

But 2 Samuel 12 records in a poignant verse what happened after the death of that child: "David comforted his wife Bathsheba, and went in to her and lay with her; and she gave birth to a son, and he named him Solomon. *Now the Lord loved him*" (v. 24, emphasis added).

Here is an explicit statement of the special love of God for an individual. The Lord *loved* Solomon. The prophet Nathan even nicknamed Solomon "Jedidiah," meaning "beloved of the Lord," to signify the Lord's love for him (v. 25).

Solomon was a newborn infant. He was not yet a believer. He had not yet done good or evil. Yet the Lord set His love on Solomon, even though he was the child of a sinful union that should never have been.

Nor was Solomon's life free from sin. Solomon was drawn to the same kind of sin that caused his father to fall. Scripture tells us Solomon took hundreds of wives. He dabbled in idolatry. Despite his great wisdom, he often behaved foolishly. One thing is certain: God did not set His love on Solomon because Solomon deserved it.

But the Lord delights in pouring out the riches of His love on undeserving sinners. He is a God of grace. He sets His love on whom He chooses, and draws them to Himself in love. Solomon, despite the abundance of sin in his life, *did* love the Lord (1 Ki. 3:3). God's love for Solomon guaranteed Solomon's love for God. "We love him, because he first loved us" (1 Jn. 4:19).

Years after Solomon, Nehemiah would return from Persia to rebuild the walls of Jerusalem. When Nehemiah discovered Israelites were marrying foreign women, he outlawed such marriages, saying, "Did not Solomon king of Israel sin regarding these things? Yet among the many nations there was no king like him, and *he was loved by his God,* and God made him king over all Israel; nevertheless the foreign women caused even him to sin" (Neh. 13:26, emphasis added).

Odd, isn't it, that in the midst of holding Solomon's sin up as a negative example not to be emulated, Nehemiah would say, "He was loved by his God"? But here's the point: God chooses to love those whom He chooses to love. He chooses *in spite of* our sin. The fact that He loves us does not mean that we are worthy. But when He chooses to love redemptively and eternally, He forgives and redeems and keeps us in the faith. His love simply will not let us go. It will bless us and chasten us and perfect us through pain—but it will never release us.

Furthermore, it is *only* by His grace that we are not left to reap the bitter consequences of our own sin. It is only by His grace that we are not *all* consumed by divine wrath (Lam. 3:22–23). People seem to get hung up asking why God did not elect everyone. But the more reasonable question is why He chose anyone at all, much less a great multitude which no man can number (cf. Rev. 7:9).

Someone will say, "But how can I know if I'm chosen?"

Do you believe? Do you love the Lord Jesus Christ and trust Him alone (not your own good deeds) to save you? Do you believe that He came into the world as God in human flesh? That He died on a cross as an atonement for sins and rose again the third day? Do you believe that He is the only one who can erase your guilt and enable you to be forgiven and clothed in righteousness? Then you were chosen to be loved everlastingly.

The particular love of God for His own is overwhelming. It is powerful. If you don't stand in awe of it, then you don't really grasp its significance.

We ought to be in awe, and like Israel, humiliated before such love. We have no right to God's love. He does not owe it to us. Yet He condescends to love us nonetheless. If our hearts aren't stirred with love for God in return, then there's something terribly wrong with us.

No wonder Paul told the Ephesians,

> For this reason, I bow my knees before the Father, from whom every family in heaven and on earth derives its name, that He would grant you, according to the riches of His

glory, to be strengthened with power through His Spirit in the inner man; so that Christ may dwell in your hearts through faith; and that you, being rooted and grounded in love, may be able to comprehend with all the saints what is the breadth and length and height and depth, and to know the love of Christ which surpasses knowledge, that you may be filled up to all the fulness of God (Eph. 3:14–19).

Finding Security in the Love of God

The Illustration: The Prodigal Son

The Doctrine: Romans 8

The Conclusion: Nothing Can Separate Us
from the Love of God in Christ Jesus

The Sum of It All: God Is Love

Chapter 8

Finding Security in the Love of God

GEORGE MATHESON, a brilliant nineteenth-century Scottish pastor and hymn writer, was born with an eye defect that developed into total blindness by the time he was eighteen. Shortly thereafter, his fiancée left him, deciding she would not be content to be married to a blind man. And so it was in response to one of the gloomiest episodes of his life that Matheson penned his great hymn about the security of God's love, "O Love that Wilt Not Let Me Go." Spurned by what he thought was true love, he sought—and found—solace in the unchanging love of God:

> *O love that wilt not let me go,*
> *I rest my weary soul in thee.*
> *I give thee back the life I owe*
> *That in thine ocean-depths its flow*
> *May richer, fuller be.*

God's love for His own simply has no parallel in human experience. As we have seen, it is a powerful, immutable love that extends from eternity past to eternity future. It is a love that is not deterred by our race's sinful rebellion against God. Because of this love God pursues and redeems us even when we are morally and spiritually reprehensible and unworthy of His love in every way: "God demonstrates His own love toward us, in that while we were yet sinners, Christ died for us" (Rom. 5:8).

In other words, God's love is so great that He would stop at nothing to redeem those whom He loved—even though it meant giving His own beloved Son. In fact, the love of God is the supreme guarantee of the believer's security. Many passages of Scripture explicitly teach this. In this chapter, I want to examine two key passages that highlight the security that is to be found in God's love. One of these is an illustration of God's love by way of a parable; the other is a doctrinal treatment extolling the security of divine love.

The Illustration: The Prodigal Son

WE BEGIN BY LOOKING at the most familiar parable of all—the parable of The Prodigal Son, found in Luke 15. The parable's centerpiece is actually not the son's prodigality, but the father's longing love and ready forgiveness for a wayward son:

> A certain man had two sons; and the younger of them said to his father, "Father, give me the share of the estate that falls to me." And he divided his wealth between them. And not many days later, the younger son gathered everything together and went on a journey into a distant country, and there he squandered his estate with loose living.
>
> Now when he had spent everything, a severe famine occurred in that country, and he began to be in need. And he went and attached himself to one of the citizens of that country, and he sent him into his fields to feed swine. And he was longing to fill his stomach with the pods that the swine were eating, and no one was giving anything to him.
>
> But when he came to his senses, he said, "How many of my father's hired men have more than enough bread, but I

am dying here with hunger! I will get up and go to my father, and will say to him, "'Father, I have sinned against heaven, and in your sight; I am no longer worthy to be called your son; make me as one of your hired men.'" And he got up and came to his father. But while he was still a long way off, his father saw him, and felt compassion for him, and ran and embraced him, and kissed him (Lk. 15:11–20).

The father represents God. The younger son is the irreligious, worldly sinner. He represents the sinner who squanders everything he has in a dissolute, irreligious life. He takes everything good his father has ever given him, spurns the father himself, and fritters away his entire legacy in loose living, immorality, and drunkenness.

He finally comes to a point in the midst of his debauchery where he realizes he has hit bottom. He's serving pig slop—hardly an acceptable job for a Jewish son—and worse, he is reduced to taking his own meals from the slop he feeds to the hogs.

Suddenly, he realizes that this is no way to live. He decides to come home. He represents the penitent sinner. He is sorrowful over his wasted life, grieving that he has squandered all his father's goodness, and very aware that he has spent his youth fruitlessly on wickedness and dissipation. He is humiliated. He knows precisely where he stands. He has had his fill of iniquity. Perhaps he once felt that facing up to his sin before his father would cost him everything; but now he knows he has nothing left to lose. He decides to go back and make things right with his father—or at least throw himself on his father's mercy.

The father's response illustrates God's love toward a penitent sinner. Even while the profligate boy is still a long way off, the father sees him (which means the father must have been looking for his wayward son). He "ran and embraced him, and kissed him" (v. 20). The verb tense indicates that he kissed him over and over. Here is tender mercy. Here is forgiveness. Here is compassion. Here is a father treating the son as if there were no past, as if his sins had been buried in the depths of the deepest sea, removed as far as the east is from the west, and forgotten. Here is unrestrained affection, unconditional love.

The father's response is remarkable. There is no diffidence. There is no hesitation. There is no withholding of emotion, no subtle coolness. There is only sympathetic, eager, pure, unbridled love. The father loves his wayward child lavishly. He loves him profusely. He loves him grandly.

The son seems shocked by this. He begins the speech he had rehearsed: "Father, I have sinned against heaven and in your sight; I am no longer worthy to be called your son" (v. 21). It's almost as if he can't deal with his father's tender affection. He is consumed by his own sense of unworthiness. He is in the throes of profound humiliation. He is fully aware of the seriousness of his sin. After all, he had been reduced to eating with pigs. Now, being showered with a loving father's kisses must have only increased his sense of utter shame.

The father's grace was, if anything, even more humbling than the prodigal son's awareness of his own sin. The young man knew in his heart that he was completely undeserving. And so he confessed, "I am no longer worthy to be called your son."

But here we are concerned primarily with the father's response. Notice that he doesn't even respond to the son's hesitancy:

> But the father said to his slaves, "Quickly bring out the best robe and put it on him, and put a ring on his hand and sandals on his feet; and bring the fattened calf, kill it, and let us eat and be merry; for this son of mine was dead, and has come to life again; he was lost, and has been found." And they began to be merry (vv. 22–24).

He pays no attention whatsoever to the penitent young man's confession of unworthiness. He just orders his servants to start the celebration. He showers the prodigal son with favors. He gives him the best robe. He puts a ring on his hand. He gets sandals for his feet. And he kills the fatted calf.

There's much more that could be said about this parable, of course. There are rich spiritual lessons to be drawn from the nature of the prodigal's repentance, the response of the elder brother, and many other aspects of the parable. But the point that interests us here is how Jesus pictured the love of God toward a penitent sinner.

God's love is like the love of this father. It is not minimal; it is unreserved. It is unrestrained. It is extravagant. It is not bestowed in moderation. There is no holding back—just pure love undiluted, without any resentment or disaffection. The father receives the wayward boy as a privileged son, not as a lowly servant.

Above all, the love of the father was an unconditional love. It was undiminished by the rebellion of the son. Despite all that this boy had done to deserve his father's wrath, the father responded with unrestrained love. Though the young man may not have realized it while he was languishing in the far country, he could not be estranged from so loving a father. Even his great sins could not ultimately separate him from his father's love.

The apostle Paul taught a similar lesson in one of the great doctrinal sections of Scripture—Romans 8:31–39. That passage makes a fitting climax for our study.

The Doctrine: Romans 8

ALL THE WRITINGS of the apostle Paul are didactic and doctrinal. Most of his epistles begin with a section of pure doctrine and culminate with a section of practical application. The book of Romans is Paul's great treatise on justification by faith. The doctrinal section of this book is a full, systematic, logical exposition of the doctrine of justification. It reaches its pinnacle at the end of Romans 8, where Paul discusses the security of the believer:

The God Who Loves

> What then shall we say to these things? If God is for us, who is against us? He who did not spare His own Son, but delivered Him up for us all, how will He not also with Him freely give us all things? Who will bring a charge against God's elect? God is the one who justifies; who is the one who condemns? Christ Jesus is He who died, yes, rather who was raised, who is at the right hand of God, who also intercedes for us (Rom. 8:31–34).

Let's set this passage in its immediate context: One of the main themes of Romans 8 is that salvation is entirely God's work. Verses 7–8 declare the hopeless state of every unredeemed person: "The mind set on the flesh is hostile toward God; for it does not subject itself to the law of God, for it is not even able to do so; and those who are in the flesh cannot please God." The sinner is therefore trapped in his own insuperable lostness, unless God intervenes to save him.

And as Paul states, that is precisely what happens. God Himself orchestrates salvation from eternity past to eternity future: "Whom He foreknew, He also predestined to become conformed to the image of His Son, that He might be the first-born among many brethren; and whom He predestined, these He also called; and whom He called, these He also justified; and whom He justified, these He also glorified" (vv. 29–30).

Every stage of the process is God's work. There's a tremendous amount of security in that. If our salvation is God's work, not our own, we can be sure that He will see it to full fruition. "He who began a good work in you will perfect it until the day of Christ Jesus" (Phil. 1:6). Believers are "protected by the power of God through faith for a salvation ready to be revealed in the last time" (1 Pet. 1:5). God is both the Author and the Finisher of our salvation, and He personally guarantees that we will persevere in faith to the end.

That does not mean, incidentally, that believers will never fall into sin. We know from the lives of saints such as David and

Solomon that it is possible for believers to sin in shameful ways. But what is guaranteed is that no true believer can ever fall away totally and finally from the faith. Genuine believers cannot lapse into unbelief. They cannot turn from Christ completely. God will discipline His children who sin (Heb. 12:7–8), but even that discipline is a token of God's love, not His wrath: "For those whom the Lord loves He disciplines, and He scourges every son whom He receives" (Heb. 12:6). True believers can never be separated from the love of God. God Himself guarantees it. As Jesus said, "I give eternal life to them, and they shall never perish; and no one shall snatch them out of My hand. My Father, who has given them to Me, is greater than all; and no one is able to snatch them out of the Father's hand" (Jn. 10:28–29).

Professing believers who do fall away only prove that their faith was never genuine to begin with: "They went out from us, but they were not really of us; for if they had been of us, they would have remained with us; but they went out, in order that it might be shown that they all are not of us" (1 Jn. 2:19). That verse speaks not of people who fall into temptation and sin, but of those who fall away totally and finally from the faith. These are people who utterly abandon the faith. True believers are not capable of such spiritual treachery. God graciously and lovingly insures their perseverance. Like Peter, we can be sifted like wheat, but if our faith is genuine, it will not fail (cf. Lk. 22:31–32).

Here in Romans 8, Paul declares that God's love is the greatest guarantee that every true believer will persevere in the faith. He uses a succession of arguments, all based on the truth that salvation is solely God's work.

God Is for Us

"WHAT THEN SHALL WE SAY to these things? If God is for us, who is against us?" (v. 31). The argument is simple: If God is working to save us, nothing will thwart the work. Whatever God undertakes will most certainly be accomplished. And if God is on our side, it doesn't matter who is on the other side. God's side will be victorious. If God is for us, no one can stand against us.

Someone has said that God plus one equals a majority. The truth is that God alone makes a majority. If every creature in the material and immaterial universe combined to oppose God together, still He would not be defeated. He is infinitely greater, and holier, and wiser, and more powerful than the aggregate of all His creation.

So the fact that He is working to save me makes the outcome certain. If my salvation were ultimately up to me, I would have much to fear. If my redemption hinged in any way on my abilities, I would be lost. Like any sinner, I'm prone to disobedience, unbelief, and weakness. If it were up to me alone to keep myself in the love of God, I would surely fail.

At this point someone might point out that Jude 21 does say, "Keep yourselves in the love of God." Does that mean we're dependent on our own staying power to remain within the purview of God's love? Of course not. Jude acknowledges just three verses later that only God "is able to keep you from stumbling, and to make you stand in the presence of His glory blameless with great joy" (v. 24).

And with God on our side, Paul says, no one can stand against us. This echoes a recurring theme of the Psalms. David wrote, "The Lord is my light and my salvation; whom shall I fear? The Lord is the defense of my life; whom shall I dread?" (Ps. 27:1). Psalm 46 says, "God is our refuge and strength, a very present help in trouble. Therefore we will not fear. . . . The Lord of hosts is with us; the God of Jacob is our stronghold" (vv. 1–2, 11). And the repeated refrain of Psalm 80 suggests that when the Lord causes His face to shine upon us, *we will be saved* (vv. 3, 7, 19, emphasis added). No doubt about it. When the Lord sets out to accomplish something, who can oppose Him?

If anyone could rob us of our salvation, that person would have to be greater than God Himself. God is for us. He has set His love on us. No human, no angel, not even Satan himself can alter that. So if God is for us, it matters not who is against us.

Yes, someone says, but can't Christians put themselves outside God's grace? What about those who commit abominable sins? Don't they nullify the work of redemption in themselves? Don't they forfeit the love of God?

Certainly not. That kind of thinking posits an impossible situation. Remember that we did not gain salvation by our own efforts, so it's preposterous to think that we can forfeit it by anything we do. We did not choose God in the first place; He chose us (Jn. 15:16). We are drawn to Christ only by God's redeeming love (Jer. 31:3). His love continues to draw us and hold us. This is Paul's very point in Romans 8. God's love guarantees our security. That same love also guarantees our perseverance. "We love him, because he first loved us" (1 Jn. 4:19, KJV). Now "The love of Christ controls us" (2 Cor. 5:14). And we continue in the faith because we are protected by His power (1 Pet. 1:5). Thus, His own love insures that we cannot do anything to remove ourselves from His grace.

We can no more forfeit the love of God than the prodigal son could destroy his father's love for him. Like the father of the prodigal son, God loves us constantly. He forgives eagerly, loves lavishly, and does not deal with us according to our sins, or reward us according to our iniquities (Ps. 103:10). Moreover, He does something the prodigal son's father could not do: He sovereignly draws us to Himself. His love is like a cord that draws us inexorably to Him (Hos. 11:4). "He chose us in [Christ] before the foundation of the world, that we should be holy and blameless before Him. In love He predestined us to adoption as sons through Jesus Christ to Himself, according to the kind intention of His will" (Eph. 1:4–5). And "whom He predestined . . . these He also glorified" (Rom. 8:30). He sees the process through to the end.

Our salvation is the work of God. God is "for us," and no one can deter Him from accomplishing what He has determined to do.

The God Who Loves

Christ Died for Us

HERE'S MORE PROOF that we are eternally secure: "He who did not spare His own Son, but delivered Him up for us all, how will He not also with Him freely give us all things?" (Rom. 8:32). God loves us regardless of the cost. Consider what God's love for us has already cost Him: He gave His own beloved Son to die in order to accomplish our salvation. Having already paid so great a price to redeem us, He won't allow the process to stop short of the goal. And if He has already given His best and dearest on our behalf, why would He withhold anything from us now?

Would God redeem sinners at the cost of His own Son's blood, then cast those same blood-bought believers aside? Having brought us to salvation at so great a price, would He then withhold any grace from us? Won't He finish what He started?

And consider this: God gave Christ to die for us "while we were yet sinners" (Rom. 5:8). Would He turn His back on us now that we are justified? If He didn't spurn us when we were rebellious sinners, would He then cast us aside now that we are His children? "If while we were enemies, we were reconciled to God through the death of His Son" (Rom. 5:10), doesn't it seem reasonable that He will do everything necessary to keep us in the fold now that we are reconciled? If He gave us grace to trust Christ in the first place, He will assuredly give grace to keep us from falling away.

Psalm 84:11 says, "For the Lord God is a sun and shield: the Lord will give grace and glory: no good thing will he withhold from them that walk uprightly." God is not stingy with His grace, and the proof of that is seen in the sacrifice of Christ on our behalf. "But he giveth more grace" (Jas. 4:6, KJV).

The sacrifice of Christ is eternally bound up in God's love for the elect. Did you know that in eternity past, before God had even begun the work of creation, He promised to redeem the elect? Titus 1:2 says the promise of eternal life was made "before the world began" (KJV)—literally, before the beginning of time. So this speaks of a divine promise made before anything was created.

Who made this promise and with whom was it made? Since it was made before creation commenced, there is only one possible answer: it was a promise made between the triune Members of the Godhead. God the Father, God the Son, and God the Spirit promised among themselves to redeem fallen humanity.

The plan of redemption was made not after Adam fell but before the beginning of creation. This is consistent with everything Scripture says about election. The saved are chosen in Christ "before the foundation of the world" (Eph. 1:4). God called us . . . in Christ Jesus from all eternity" (2 Tim. 1:9). The eternal kingdom is prepared for them "from the foundation of the world" (Matt. 25:34). Christ was foreordained to shed His blood on their behalf "before the foundation of the world" (1 Pet. 1:20). The names of the elect are written in the Book of Life "from the foundation of the world" (Rev. 13:8; 17:8).

This means the plan of redemption is no contingency. It is not Plan B. It is no alternative strategy. It *is* God's plan, the very purpose for which He created us.

Furthermore, it means that the elect are God's gift of love to His Son. That's why Christ refers to them as "those whom Thou hast given Me" (Jn. 17:9, 24; 18:9). The Father has given the elect to Christ as a gift of love, and therefore not one of them will be lost. Both the Father and the Son work together to insure the fulfillment of their eternal plan of redemption. This further assures the salvation of all the elect, for as Jesus said, "All that the Father gives Me shall come to Me, and the one who comes to Me I will certainly not cast out. . . . For this is the will of My Father, that everyone who beholds the Son and believes in Him, may have eternal life; and I Myself will raise him up on the last day" (John 6:37, 40).

So Christ Himself promises to see God's plan of redemption through to the end. Having died as a substitute for those whom the Father gave Him, He promises to see the process through to the final consummation in glory. Likewise, the Father, having already given His Son to die on our behalf, will not now withhold anything necessary to complete our redemption.

God Himself Justifies Us

REMEMBER THAT THE THEME of Paul's epistle to the Romans is justification by faith. Paul began chapter 8 with a crucial statement about justification: "There is therefore now no condemnation for those who are in Christ Jesus." There is a wealth of theology in that verse. It draws together all the threads of truth about justification that the apostle had been weaving in the preceding chapters.

Paul had been teaching the Romans that justification is a forensic event whereby God forgives the sins of those who believe and imputes to them a perfect righteousness. In chapter 4, for example, he spoke of believers as "Those whose lawless deeds have been forgiven, and whose sins have been covered" (Rom. 4:7). The Lord does not take their sins into account (v. 8). And what's more, righteousness is reckoned to their account (v. 11). Therefore, they stand before God without fear of His righteous judgment (Rom. 8:1).

All this hinges on the fact that they are "in Christ;" that is, they have been united with Him by faith. Paul has already outlined this doctrine in Romans 6:3–5.

So consider the implications of this doctrine: Those who are "in Christ" have their sins completely forgiven; they have all the merit of Christ Himself imputed to their account. God Himself has undertaken to justify them. Christ has accomplished redemption on their behalf. They stand in God's favor solely because He decided to show grace to them, not because of anything they did to earn it. Therefore, Paul asks, if God declares them not guilty, who is going to condemn them? "Who will bring a charge against

God's elect? God is the one who justifies; who is the one who condemns? (8:33–34).

There's a tremendous amount of security in the doctrine of justification by faith. It is because of this doctrine that we can rest in our salvation as an accomplished fact. Jesus said, "Truly, truly, I say to you, he who hears My word, and believes Him who sent Me, has eternal life, and does not come into judgment, but has passed out of death into life" (Jn. 5:24, emphasis added). As Paul says, *"There is therefore now no condemnation for those who are in Christ Jesus"* (Rom. 8:1, emphasis added). It is a done deal, not a goal we work toward. Eternal life is a present possession, not a future hope. And our justification is a declaration that takes place in the court of heaven, so no earthly judge can alter the verdict. When God Himself says "not guilty," who can say otherwise?

Our Heavenly High Priest Intercedes for Us

THE ONGOING WORK OF CHRIST is yet another reason we cannot fall out of favor with God. Paul writes, "Christ Jesus is He who died, yes, rather who was raised, who is at the right hand of God, who also intercedes for us" (v. 34).

Did you realize that Jesus makes continuous intercession for all believers? Hebrews 7:25, echoing Paul's thought in Romans 8:34, says, "He is able to save forever those who draw near to God through Him, since He always lives to make intercession for them." Jesus' ongoing intercession on our behalf guarantees our salvation "forever"—literally, to the uttermost.

How does Christ pray on our behalf? Surely what He prays is similar to the great high priestly prayer recorded in John 17. He prays for our security (Jn. 17:11–12). He prays that we might be in the world but not of the world (vv. 14–15). He prays that we might be kept from evil (v. 15). He prays for our sanctification (v. 17). He prays that we will be one with Him, one with the Father, and one with one another (vv. 21–23). In short, He is praying that we will be kept in the faith, that we might "never perish," and that no one would snatch us out of His hand (John 10:28).

Will that prayer be answered? Certainly. In fact, to deny that the believer is secure in Christ and secure in the love of God, is to deny that Christ's priestly work is sufficient. And to doubt whether the believer might fall out of favor with God is to misunderstand God's love for His elect.

The Conclusion: Nothing Can Separate Us from the Love of God in Christ Jesus

THE ENERGY that has driven God's plan of redemption from eternity past flows from the power of His love. He chose us and predestined us "in love" (Eph. 1:4–5). It is solely "because of His great love with which He loved us" that He raised us from our hopeless state of spiritual death (Eph. 2:4). It is because He loved us with an everlasting love that He drew us to Himself (Jer. 31:3). Christ died because of God's love for us (Rom. 5:8).

In other words, election is the highest expression of God's love to sinful humanity. Some people hate this doctrine. They fight against it, try to explain it away, or claim it's not fair. Some even claim it is a form of tyranny, or that it is fatalistic, or that it violates the human will. But in reality the doctrine of election is all about the eternal, inviolable love of God.

Is it tyranny? Certainly not. God's sovereignty is not the sovereignty of a tyrant, but the loving providence of a gracious God. As we have seen, He finds no pleasure in the destruction of the wicked, but pleads with them to repent and turn to Him for mercy (Ezek. 33:11). He showers blessings on the wicked *and* the righteous alike (Matt. 5:45). His very goodness is an appeal to the wicked that they should repent (Rom. 2:4). He weeps over those who refuse His mercies (Lk. 13:34). Why does He not elect everyone for salvation? We are not told, but the answer is certainly not because of any deficiency or lack in God's love.

What about the charge that the doctrine of election is fatalism? B. B. Warfield said this charge is usually leveled by people who "wish to be the architects of their own fortunes, the determiners of their own destinies; though why they should fancy they could do that better for themselves than God can be trusted to do it for them, it puzzles one to understand."[1] Fatalism is the notion that all things are controlled by an impersonal or irrational force—Fate. God is sovereign, but He is by no means impersonal or irrational. The difference between fatalism and the biblical doctrine of divine sovereignty is really quite profound. It is true, as Scripture teaches, that God "works all things after the counsel of His will" (Eph. 1:11), and that He will accomplish all His good pleasure (Isa. 46:10). But He does not govern arbitrarily or whimsically.

Nor does God impose His sovereign will in a way that does violence to the will of the creature.[2] The outworking of His eternal plan in no way restricts the liberty of our choices or diminishes our responsibility when we make wrong choices. Unbelief is forced on no one. Those who go to a Christless eternity make their own choice in accord with their own desires. They are not under any compulsion from God to sin. "Let no one say when he is tempted, 'I am being tempted by God'; for God cannot be tempted by evil, and He Himself does not tempt anyone" (Jas. 1:13). People who choose unbelief make that choice in full accord with their own desires.

What about the charge that the doctrine of election is not fair? In one sense, there's some truth in this. "Fair" would mean that everyone gets precisely what he deserves. But no one really wants that. Even the non-elect would face a more severe punishment if it were not for the restraining grace of God that keeps them from expressing their depravity to its full extent.

Fairness is not the issue; *grace* is the issue. Election is the highest expression of God's loving grace. He didn't have to choose anyone. And He is, after all, God. If He chooses to set His love in a particular way on whomever He chooses, He has every right to do so.

But for Christians, the knowledge that we are saved because of God's choice is the supreme source of security. If God loved us from eternity past, and He is unchanging, then we can know that His love for us in eternity future will be undiminished.

This is precisely Paul's point in Romans 8 as he wraps up his discourse on the believer's security. The closing verses of this passage read like a hymn on the love of God:

> Who shall separate us from the love of Christ? Shall tribulation, or distress, or persecution, or famine, or nakedness, or peril, or sword? Just as it is written, "For Thy sake we are being put to death all day long; we were considered as sheep to be slaughtered." But in all these things we overwhelmingly conquer through Him who loved us. For I am convinced that neither death, nor life, nor angels, nor principalities, nor things present, nor things to come, nor powers, nor height, nor depth, nor any other created thing, shall be able to separate us from the love of God, which is in Christ Jesus our Lord (Rom. 8:35–39).

Writing to the Ephesians, Paul described the Christian life as spiritual warfare. "Our struggle is not against flesh and blood, but against the rulers, against the powers, against the world forces of this darkness, against the spiritual forces of wickedness in the heavenly places" (Eph. 6:12). Wicked forces, diabolical persons, and evil circumstances all conspire to attack each believer. At times it seems as if all the forces of hell are arrayed against us. That would be daunting, except as Paul points out in Romans 8, the outcome is guaranteed.

Nothing can separate us from the love of God in Christ—not earthly trials, such as "tribulation, or distress, or persecution, or famine, or nakedness, or peril, or sword" (v. 35), and not even heavenly foes—"neither death, nor life, nor angels, nor principalities, nor things present, nor things to come, nor powers, nor height, nor depth, nor any other created thing" (vv. 38–39). "In all these things we overwhelmingly conquer through Him who loved us" (v. 37). It's a no-lose situation—because of the love of God.

The various threats Paul outlined were not hypothetical dilemmas as far as he was concerned. Tribulation, distress, persecution, famine, sword—Paul had faced those very hardships—and others as well.

> . . . beaten times without number, often in danger of death. Five times I received from the Jews thirty-nine lashes. Three times I was beaten with rods, once I was stoned, three times I was shipwrecked, a night and a day I have spent in the deep. I have been on frequent journeys, in dangers from rivers, dangers from robbers, dangers from my countrymen, dangers from the Gentiles, dangers in the city, dangers in the wilderness, dangers on the sea, dangers among false brethren; I have been in labor and hardship, through many sleepless nights, in hunger and thirst, often without food, in cold and exposure (2 Cor. 11:23–27).

And Paul had emerged from those trials with an unshaken confidence in the love of God.

The people of God have always suffered. In Romans 8:36 Paul quotes Psalm 44:22 by way of reminder: "For Thy sake we are killed all day long; we are considered as sheep to be slaughtered." God's love does not necessarily guarantee earthly comfort. But the sufferings of this world are more than compensated by the rewards of divine love in eternal bliss. As Paul wrote earlier in Romans 8, "I consider that the sufferings of this present time are not worthy to be compared with the glory that is to be revealed to us" (v. 18; cf. 2 Cor. 4:17).

"The glory that is to be revealed to us" is God's glory. As we said at the close of chapter 5, every aspect of God's love declares His glory. The general love God has toward all humanity reveals

His basic goodness. The fact that it is spurned by those who do not believe in no way diminishes God's glory. Even the wrath of sinful men shall praise Him (Ps. 76:10).

But the riches of His goodness and glory are revealed most clearly in the salvation of the elect, a great multitude that no man could ever number (Rev. 7:9).

"This hope we have as an anchor of the soul, a hope both sure and steadfast" (Heb. 6:19).

The Sum of It All: God Is Love

GOD IS LOVE. His mercy is over all His works. He manifests His love to all. But the highest expression of His love is manifest to those who by sheer grace He lovingly draws to Himself.

Therefore to those of us who believe, God's love is a uniquely precious reality, albeit an unfathomable one. There is no way we can scale the height of it. There is no way we can imagine the breadth of it or span the width of it. Nevertheless, by God's grace we can know the love of Christ, which passes knowledge (Eph. 3:18–19).

We daily benefit from the goodness of His love. He gives us richly all things to enjoy (1 Tim. 6:17). More than that, His love is shed abroad in our own hearts (Rom. 5:5). I know of no greater source of comfort, no more sure foundation for our security, no richer source of contentment.

Why is all this so important? Ultimately the love of God is the basis for all our hopes. It is the object of our deepest longings. It is the source and fulfillment of our faith. It is the very basis for His grace to us. After all, we love Him only because He first loved us (1 Jn. 4:19). And His love is also our guarantee of eternal bliss. Since He loved us enough to send His own Son to die for us while we were yet His enemies—we have no reason to fear losing that love, now that His Spirit has been sent forth into our hearts, enabling us to cry, "Abba, Father!" (Gal. 4:5). His love absolutely permeates and envelops every aspect of our lives in Christ.

As Christians, then, we ought to see that everything we enjoy in life—from our tiniest pleasures to the eternal redemption we have found in Christ—is an expression of the great love wherewith God loved us (Eph. 2:4). The blessing of His love comes to us not because we deserve it, but simply and only because of His sovereign grace. For certainly we do not deserve His blessing, but the very opposite. Yet He pours out His love without measure, and we are invited to partake of its benefits freely.

As recipients of love like that, we can only fall on our faces in wonder. When we contemplate such love, it ought to make us feel unworthy. Yet at the same time it lifts us to unimaginable heights of joy and confidence, because we know that our God, the righteous judge of all the universe, the One to whom we have by faith committed our very souls' well-being—has revealed Himself as a God of immeasurable love. And *we* are the objects of that love—despite our unworthiness and despite our sin! In light of the glories of divine love, how can we not be utterly lost in wonder, love, and praise?

Appendices

Appendix 1: Fury Not in God

Appendix 2: On the Love of God, and Whether it Extends to the Non-Elect

Appendix 3: Christ the Savior of the World

Appendix 4: The Love of God to the World

Appendix 1

Fury Not in God

EDITOR'S NOTE: This classic tract by Thomas Chalmers, a Glasgow pastor and professor of theology at the University of Edinburgh in the first half of the 1800s, was adapted from one of his best-known sermons.

All Scripture references in this Appendix are from the King James Version of the Bible.

"Fury is not in me: who would set the briers and thorns against me in battle? I would go through them, I would burn them together. Or let him take hold of my strength, that he may make peace with me; and he shall make peace with me" (Isaiah 27:4–5).

THERE ARE THREE DISTINCT LESSONS in this text. The first, that fury is not in God; the second, that He does not want to glorify Himself by the death of sinners ("Who would set the briers and thorns against me in battle?"); the third, the invitation ("Take hold of my strength, that you may make peace with me; and you shall make peace with me").

The God Who Loves

Fury Is Not in God

"FURY IS NOT IN ME," the Lord states. But how can this be? Isn't fury one manifestation of His essential attributes? Do we not repeatedly read of His fury—of His fury being poured forth in the streets of Jerusalem (Jer. 44:6); of God casting the fury of His wrath upon the world (Job 20:23); of Him rendering His anger upon His enemies with fury (Isa. 59:18); of Him kindling the fire of His fury in Zion (Lam. 4:11); of Him pouring out His fury like a fire (Lam. 2:4)? We are not therefore to think that fury is banished altogether from God's administration. There are occasions when this fury is discharged against the objects of God's wrath; and there must be other times when there is no fury in Him.

Now what is the occasion our text refers to when He disclaims all fury? He is inviting men to reconciliation. He is calling them to make peace with Him. He is assuring them that if they will only take hold of His strength, they can make peace with Him.

In the preceding verses, the Lord speaks of a vineyard. When He invites people to lay hold of His strength, He is in fact inviting those who are outside the boundaries of the vineyard to enter in. Fury will be discharged on those who reject the invitation. But we cannot say that there is any exercise of fury in God at the time of giving the invitation. In fact, our text explicitly and directly states God's assurance to the contrary.

Instead of fury, there is a longing desire after you. There is a wish to save you from that awful day in which the fury of a rejected Savior will be spread abroad over all who have despised Him. The tone of God's invitation is not a tone of anger—it is a tone of tenderness. The look that accompanies the invitation is not a look of wrath—it is a look of affection. There will certainly be an occasion when the fury of God will be poured forth on those who have held out against Him and turned away in unbelief and contempt from His beseeching voice. But while He is lifting this voice—while He is sending messengers over the face of the earth to circulate His gracious invitation among the habitations of men—especially at this time, when Bibles are within the reach of every family and ministers in every pulpit are sounding forth the overtures of the gospel—surely at such a time and upon such an occasion, it may well be said of God to all who are now seeking His face and favor, that there is no fury in Him.

It is just as in the parable of the marriage feast many rejected the king's invitation (Matt. 22:2–7). The king was rightfully angry with many of them, and sent forth his armies and destroyed them, and burned up their city (v. 7). On that occasion there was fury in the king, and on the like occasion will there be fury in God. But He can truthfully say at the time when He is now giving the invitation, "Fury is not in Me."

In His invitation is kindness, a desire for peace and friendship, and a longing earnestness to erase the enmity which now exists between the Lawgiver in heaven and His yet impenitent and unreconciled creatures.

This very process was all gone through before the destruction of Jerusalem. Israel rejected the warnings and invitations of the Savior, and at length experienced His fury. But there was no fury at the time of His giving the invitations. The tone of our Savior's voice when He uttered "O Jerusalem, Jerusalem" (Lk. 13:34) was not the tone of a vindictive and irritated fury. There was compassion in it—a warning and pleading earnestness that they would repent and make peace with God. He testified that He would willingly have gathered them as a hen gathers her chickens under her wings, so it may well be said that there was no fury in the Son of God, no fury in God.

Let's make the application to ourselves in the present day. On the last day there will be a tremendous discharge of fury. All the wrath that sinners are now treasuring up will be poured forth on them. The season of God's mercy will then have come to an end. After the sound of the last trumpet, there will nevermore be heard the sounding call of reconciliation. Oh, my brethren, God will in the last day pour forth His wrath in one mighty torrent on the heads of the impenitent. That wrath is now gathering and accumulating in a storehouse of vengeance; and at some awful point in the future, when time shall be no more, the door of that storehouse will be opened and the fury of the Lord will break loose against the guilty. Then His righteous fury will execute the full weight and the terror of all His threatenings.

Therefore, my brethren, you misunderstand the text if you infer from it that fury has no place in the history or methods of God's administration. God's wrath does have its time and its occasion. And the very greatest display of it is yet to come, when "the heavens shall pass away with a great noise, and the elements shall melt with fervent heat, the earth also and the works that are therein shall be burned up" (2 Pet. 3:10). In that day, "the Lord Jesus shall be revealed from heaven with his mighty angels, in flaming fire taking vengeance on them that know not God, and that obey not the gospel of our Lord Jesus Christ: Who shall be punished with everlasting destruction from the presence of the Lord, and from the glory of his power" (2 Thess. 1:7–9).

It makes one shudder seriously to think that there may be some reading these words whom the devouring torrent of divine wrath shall sweep away. Some who read these words will be drawn into the whirl of destruction, and forced to take their descending way through the mouth of that pit where the worm dies not, and the fire is not quenched. In fact, some foolishly presume there is no fury in God whatsoever, or at any time. Tragically, they will discover throughout the dreary extent of one hopeless and endless and unmitigated eternity, that God's fury is the only attribute of His they will ever really know.

So hear me. Hear me before you take your bed in hell. Hear me before that prison door be shut against you never, never again to be opened. Hear me before the great day of the revelation of God's wrath comes around, and there shall be a total breaking up of the system that now looks so stable and so unalterable. On that awful day we will not be able to take up the text and say there is no fury in God.

But hear me now—for your lives, hear me. On this day I can say it. At this moment I can throw abroad among you the wide announcement that there is no fury in God. There is not one of you into whose heart this announcement may not enter. You will be welcome to make eternal peace with your beseeching God. Surely as long as I am called by God to hold out the language of entreaty, and to sound in your ears the tidings of gladness, and to invite you to enter into the vineyard of God—surely when the messenger of the gospel is thus executing the commission with which he is charged and warranted, he may well say that there is no fury in God. Surely when the Son of God is inviting you to kiss Him and to enter into reconciliation, there is neither the feeling nor the exercise of fury.

It is only if you refuse, and if you persist in refusing, and if you suffer all these calls and entreaties to be lost upon you—it is only then that God will execute His fury and put forth the power of His anger. And therefore He says to us, "Kiss the Son, lest he be angry, and ye perish from the way, when his wrath is kindled but a little. Blessed are all they that put their trust in him" (Ps. 2:12).

This, then, is the point of time at which you stand: there is no fury in God; in fact, He is inviting you to flee from it. He is uttering no blasting curse upon the fig tree (cf. Matt. 21:19–20), even though it has so far borne no fruit. Instead, He says, "Let it alone this year also, till I shall dig about it, and dung it: and if it bear fruit, well: and if not, then after that thou shalt cut it down" (Lk. 13:8–9).

Now, my brethren, you are all in the situation of this fig tree. You are for the present let alone. God has purposes of kindness toward every one of you; and as one of His ministers, I can now say to all who read this that there is no fury in God. When the proclaimer of the good news is trying to soften your hearts, he is warranted to make full use of the argument of my text—that there is no fury in God.

The God Who Loves

When the ambassador of Christ is imploring you with the offers of grace, he is surely charged with matter of far different import from wrath and threatening and vengeance. Oh, let not all this pleading turn out to be unavailing! Let not the offer be made now, and no fruit appear afterwards; let not yours be the fate of the barren and unfruitful fig tree.

The day of the fury of the Lord is approaching. The burning up of this earth and the passing away of these heavens is an event to which we are continually drawing nearer. On that day when the whole of the universe shall be turned into a heap of ruins, we shall see the gleam of a mighty conflagration. We shall hear the noise of the framework of creation rending into fragments. On that day a cry shall be raised from a despairing multitude from all generations who have just awoke from their resting places. The terror at His wrath on that day will be more horrible than all the rest of the destruction of the universe.

Oh, my brethren, on that day the Judge will appear charged with the mighty object of vindicating before men and angels the truth and the majesty of God. And on that day the fury of God will appear in a bright and burning manifestation.

But what I have to tell you on this day is this: such fury is not now in God. Now is an opportunity to make peace with God for all eternity. And if you will only hear on this the day of your merciful visitation, you will be borne off in safety from all those horrors. Amid the wild war and frenzy of the reeling elements of divine judgment, you will be carried by the arms of love to a place of security and everlasting triumph.

God Is Not Wanting to Glorify Himself by the Death of Sinners

THAT BRINGS US TO THE second point of this text: "who would set the briers and thorns against me in battle?" Both the wicked and the righteous are often represented in Scripture by figures from the plant kingdom. For example, the saved and sanctified are called trees of righteousness, planted by the Lord that He might be glorified (Isa. 61:3). The godly man is said to be like a tree planted by the rivers of water, bringing forth its fruit in its season (Ps. 1:3). The judgment that comes upon a man is compared to an ax laid to the root of a tree (Matt. 3:10). A tree is said to be known by its fruit, and as a proof that the character of men is symbolized by the tree, we read, "of thorns men do not gather figs, nor of a bramble bush gather they grapes" (Lk. 6:44).

Observe that the thorn is specifically referred to in our text from Isaiah 27:4–5. When God says, "I would go through them, I would burn them together," He speaks of the destruction that comes on all who remain in the state of thorns and briers. This agrees with what we read in Hebrews 6:8: "that which beareth thorns and briers is rejected, and is nigh unto cursing; whose end is to be burned."

Thorns and briers are in other places even more directly employed to signify the enemies of God. "And the light of Israel shall be for a fire," says Isaiah 17:10, "and his Holy One for a flame: and it shall burn and devour his thorns and his briers in one day."

Therefore, when God says, "Who would set the briers and thorns against me in battle? I would go through them, I would burn them together," He speaks of the ease with which He could accomplish His wrath upon His enemies. They would perish before Him like the moth. They could not stand the lifting up of the red right arm of the displeasure of Almighty God.

Why set up, then, a contest so unequal as this? Why put the wicked in battle array against Him who could go through them and devour them in an instant by the breath of His fury? *God is saying in the text that this is not what He is wanting.* He does not want to set Himself forth as an enemy, or as a strong man armed against them for the battle—it is a battle He is not at all disposed to enter into. The glory He would achieve by a victory over a host so feeble is not a glory that His heart is at all set upon.

Oh, no, children of men! He has no pleasure in your death. He is not seeking to magnify Himself by the destruction of so paltry a foe. He could devour you in a moment. He could burn you up like stubble. And you are mistaken if you think renown on so poor a field of contest is a renown that He aspires after.

Who would set the grasshoppers in battle array against the giants? Who would set thorns and briers in battle array against God? This is not what He wants. He would rather something else. Be assured, He would rather you turn, and live, and come into His vineyard, and submit to Him in faith, and receive His offer of mercy. In the language of verse 5, He would rather that sinners take hold of His strength and make peace with Him.

Now tell me if this does not open up a most wonderful and a most inviting view of God? It is the real attitude in which He puts Himself forth in the gospel of His Son. It is why He says, in the hearing of all to whom the Word of this salvation is sent, "*Why will ye die?*" (Ezek. 18:31).

It is true that by the death of a sinner God *could* manifest the dignity of His Godhead. He *could* make known the power of His wrath. He *could* spread the awe of His truth and His majesty over the whole territory of His government, and send forth to its uttermost limits the glories of His strength and His immutable sovereignty. But He does not want to magnify Himself over men in this way. He has no ambition whatever after the renown of such a victory over such weak and insignificant enemies. Their resistance is no trial whatever to His strength or to His greatness. There is nothing in the destruction of creatures so weak that can at all bring Him any distinction, or throw any aggrandizement around Him. And thus we see Him pleading and protesting with sinners everywhere in Scripture. He does not want to signalize Himself upon the ruin of any, but would rather that they should turn and be saved.

And now, my dear readers, what remains for you to do? God is willing to save you. Are you willing to be saved? The way is set before you most patiently and clearly in the Bible. In fact, our very text, brief as it is, points out the way, as I shall endeavor to explain and set before you under my third point. But meanwhile, and all the better to secure a hearing from you, let me ask you to lay it upon your consciences: Are you in a state of readiness to stand before God?

If not, then I beseech you to think how certainly death will (and how speedily it may) come upon you. Even the youngest among us should be aware that death can come quickly. The agony of the parting breath will come. The time when you are stretched a lifeless corpse before the eyes of weeping relatives will come. The coffin that will enclose you will come. The hour when the company assemble to carry you to the burial ground will come. The minute when you are put into the grave will come. The throwing in of the loose earth into the narrow house where you are laid, and the spreading of the green sod over it—all, all will come on every living creature who now reads these words. In a few short years both I who now write, and you who read my words, will both be in our graves, and another generation will populate the earth.

Now you know that all this must and will happen—your common sense and common experience serve to convince you of it. Perhaps it may have been little thought of in the days of careless and thoughtless and thankless unconcern which you have spent until now. But I call on you to think of it, to lay it seriously to heart, and no longer to trifle and delay, when the high matters of death and judgment and eternity are thus set so evidently before you. This message I am commissioned to proclaim—and the blood lies on your own head and not upon mine if you will not heed the warning. The object of my message is to let you know what things are to come. It is to carry you beyond the regions of sight and of sense to the regions of faith—and to assure you, in the name of Him who cannot lie, that as surely as the hour of placing the body in the grave comes, so surely will also come the hour of the spirit returning to the God who gave it.

Yes, the day of final reckoning will also come. The appearance of the Son of God in heaven, and His mighty angels around Him, will come. The opening of the books will come. The standing of the men of all generations before the judgment seat will come. And the solemn passing of sentence that will seal your eternity will come.

Yes, and if you refuse to be reconciled in the name of Christ, now that He is beseeching you to be so, and if you refuse to turn from the evil of your ways, and to turn to your Savior in faith, I must tell you what sentence you will hear pronounced against you: "Depart from me, ye cursed, into everlasting fire, prepared for the devil and his angels" (Matt. 25:41).

There is a way of escape from the fury of this tremendous storm. There is a pathway of deliverance from the state of condemnation to the state of justification. There is a means pointed out in Scripture by which we, who by nature are the children of wrath, may come to be at peace with God. Let all ears be open then to our explanation of this way, as we bid you in the language of our text, "let him take hold of [God's] strength, that he may make peace with [Him]" (Isa. 27:5).

The Way of Salvation Is Open Before You

THE WORD *rather* signals the change between verses 4 and 5. Rather than engaging in battle with His enemies—rather than going through them and burning them with eternal destruction— God would greatly prefer that they took hold of His strength in order to make peace with Him. And He promises, as the sure effect of their turning to Him in faith, that they "shall make peace with me."

We don't have to look far to discover what this "strength" is that sinners are called to take hold of. Isaiah himself speaks of the strength of *salvation* (33:6). It is not your destruction but your salvation that God wants to put forth His strength into. Strength has already been put forth in the deliverance of a guilty world, and this is the very strength which He bids you lay hold of.

God will certainly be glorified in the destruction of the sinner, but He prefers the glory that is His through the salvation of sinners. To destroy you is to do no more than to set fire to briers and thorns and consume them. But to save you—this is indeed the power of God and the wisdom of God. This is the mighty achievement which angels desire to look into (1 Pet. 1:12). This is the enterprise upon which Christ embarked from His heavenly glory. This is the mission on which He spent all His strength and labored with distress in His soul until He accomplished it (Lk. 12:50). Now that it is accomplished, God will be glorified both in the destruction of sinners (2 Thess 1:7) and in the salvation of His saints (v. 10). But God prefers the latter to the former. He shows His wrath and makes His power known in the destruction of the sinner (Rom. 9:22). But the glory of God will redound in an even greater way forever in the eternal praise shown forth by His redeemed people (1 Pet. 2:9).

And so He pleads with you to take hold of His strength. He would greatly prefer this way of making His power known. He does not want to enter into the battle with you, or to consume you like stubble by the breath of His indignation. No; He delights to transform sinners into saints. He delights to transform vessels of wrath into vessels of mercy, and to make known the riches of His glory on those whom He had before prepared unto glory (Rom. 9:23).

There is a glorious strength put forth in the destruction of the sinner, but there is *a more glorious* strength put forth in the salvation of a sinner. This saving strength is the strength He bids you lay hold of. He would rather decline entering into a contest with sinners; for to gain a victory over them would be no more to Him than to fight with the briers and the thorns, and to consume them. But to make friends from enemies; to transform the children of wrath into children of adoption; to accomplish such a mighty and a wonderful change from the state of guilt to the state of justification; to make servants of sin into willing servants of God; to chase away the darkness of sinful nature and make everything light and comfort around the redeemed; to take people who are slaves of their feelings and invest them with a preference for the things of eternity; to pull down the strongholds of corruption within and raise one who was spiritually dead to a life of new obedience—this is the victory that God delights in! The destruction of the wicked brings Him no pleasure.

Let me now, in what remains, first say a few things more upon this strength—the strength of salvation spoken of in our text—and then allow me to state very briefly what it is to lay hold of it.

First we read of a mighty strength that had to be put forth in the work of a sinner's justification. You know that all men are sinners, and so all are under the righteous condemnation of God. How, in the name of all that is difficult and wonderful, can these sinners ever get this condemnation removed from them?

By what new and unheard of process can the guilty before God ever again become justified in His sight? How can the sentence of acquittal ever be heard on the children of iniquity from God's own throne of judgment and justice? How can God's honor be kept entire in the sight of angels, if we who have repeatedly mocked Him and insulted Him, are pardoned? How can we justly be forgiven, with all our contempt of the Law and of the Lawgiver, and with all this character of rebellion against Him written upon our foreheads? How can sinners such as we are be admitted to a place of distinction in heaven?

After all, God has committed Himself to full justice in the hearing of angels. He declared that He "will by no means clear the guilty" (Exod. 34:7). After He had given us a law by the disposition of angels, and we had not kept it, He said, "I will not justify the wicked" (Exod. 23:7). Over and over He has said things like, "The wicked shall not be unpunished" (Prov. 11:21), and, "Cursed is every one that continueth not in all things which are written in the book of the law to do them" (Gal. 3:10).

But what is more, it was not merely the good and the obedient angels who knew our rebellion. The malignant and fallen angels not only knew it, but they devised and prompted it. And how, I would ask, can God keep the awful majesty of His truth and justice entire in the sight of His adversaries, if Satan and the angels of wickedness along with him shall have it in their power to say, "We prevailed on man to insult God by sin, and now we have compelled God to put up with the affront?"

But as great as the weight and magnitude of that obstacle, so is the greatness of the strength put forth by the Savior in the mighty work of removing the obstacle. We have no adequate conception upon this matter; all we can know about it is what Scripture says. And whether we take the prophecies that foretold the work of our Redeemer, the history that recounts it, or the doctrine that expounds on its worth and its efficacy—all go to establish that there was the operation of a tremendous power in obtaining our salvation. There was the severity of a conflict; there was an arduous and mighty warfare; there were all the throes and all the exertions of a struggling (and at length a prevailing) energy in the execution of that work which our Saviour had to do. He had a barrier to surmount, and that, too, with the cries and the pains and the sorrows of heavy suffering and labor. A mighty obstacle lay before Him, and He, in the business of removing it, had to exert all the power of the faculties that belonged to Him. There was a burden laid upon His shoulders which no one else but the Prince of Peace could have borne. And there was a task placed in His hand which none but He could ever fulfil.

If all the angels in paradise had contemplated how our salvation might be accomplished, they would no doubt have concluded such a work was impossible. Who can bend the unchangeable attributes of God? Who can give them a shift so wonderful that the sinners who have insulted Him may be taken into forgiveness while His honor is kept untainted and entire? There is not one of the mighty hosts of heaven who would not have shrunk from an enterprise so lofty. Not one of them could have at once magnified the Law and released man from its violated sanctions. Not one of them could turn its threatening away from us and at the same time give truth and justice of God their brightest manifestation. Not one of them could unravel the mystery of our redemption through all the difficulties that surround it. Not one of them, by the strength of his arm, could have obtained the conquest over these difficulties.

And though you may never have contemplated such questions, let us forget not that these matters were not merely between God and man—they were between God and all the creatures He had formed. They saw the dilemma. They felt how deeply it involved the character of the Deity. They perceived its bearing on the majesty of His attributes and on the stability of the government that was upheld by Him. With them it was a matter of deep and substantial interest. And when the Eternal Son stepped forward to carry the undertaking to its end, the feeling among them all was that a battle behooved to be fought, and that the strength of this mighty Captain of our salvation alone was equal to the achievement of the victory.

Who is this that cometh from Edom, with dyed garments from Bozrah? this that is glorious in his apparel, travelling in the greatness of his strength? I that speak in righteousness, mighty to save. Wherefore art thou red in thine apparel, and thy garments like him that treadeth in the winefat? I have trodden the winepress alone; and of the people there was none with me: for I will tread them in mine anger, and trample them in my fury; and their blood shall be

sprinkled upon my garments, and I will stain all my rai-
ment. For the day of vengeance is in mine heart, and the
year of my redeemed is come. And I looked, and there was
none to help; and I wondered that there was none to
uphold: therefore mine own arm brought salvation unto
me; and my fury, it upheld me (Isa. 63:1–5).

A way of redemption has been found out in the unsearchable
riches of divine wisdom. Christ Himself is called the wisdom of
God. The same Christ is also called the power of God:

> We preach Christ crucified, unto the Jews a stumbling-
> block, and unto the Greeks foolishness; But unto them
> which are called, both Jews and Greeks, *Christ the power of
> God,* and the wisdom of God (1 Cor. 1:23–24, emphasis
> added).

In the mighty work of redemption He put forth a strength, and it
is that strength that we are called to take hold upon. There was a
wonderful strength in bearing the wrath that would have fallen
on the millions and millions more of a guilty world. There was a
strength that carried Him in triumph through the contest over
Satan, when he buffeted Him with his temptations. There was a
strength that bore Him up under the agonies of the garden. There
was a strength that supported Him when His Father's countenance was hidden from Him. There was a strength that upheld
Him in the dark hour of the travail of His soul. There was a
strength observers might think had well-nigh given way when He
called out, "My God, my God, why hast thou forsaken me?"
(Matt. 27:46).

There was a strength far greater than we know in that mysterious struggle which He held with the powers of darkness, when
Satan fell like lightning from heaven, and the Captain of our salvation spoiled principalities and powers, and made a show of

them openly, and triumphed over them. There was strength in overcoming all the mighty difficulties which lay in the way between the sinner and God, in unbarring the gates of acceptance to a guilty world, in bringing truth and mercy to meet, and right-eousness and peace to enter into fellowship—so that God might be just, while He is the justifier of him who believeth in Jesus (Rom. 3:26).

So much for the strength which is put forth in the work of man's redemption. There is also strength put forth in the work of man's sanctification. Christ has not only done a great work for us in making good our reconciliation with God—He further does a great work in us when He makes us like unto God. But I have not the time to dwell upon this last topic, and must content myself with referring you to the following Scriptures: Ephesians 1:19; 2:10; Philippians 4:13; 2 Corinthians 12:9–10; and John 15:5. The same power that raised Jesus from the dead is the power that raises us from our death in trespasses and sins. The power that was put forth on creation is the power that makes us new creatures in Jesus Christ our Lord.

Neither have I time to make out a full demonstration of what is meant by laying hold of that strength. When you apply to a friend for some service, some relief from distress or difficulty, you may be said to lay hold of him. And when you place firm reliance both on his ability and willingness to do you the service, you may well say that you have taken hold of your friend. The expression becomes all the more appropriate should *he promise* to do what you are trusting him to do. In such a case your hold is not upon his power only, but also upon his faithfulness.

And it is even so with the promises of God in Christ Jesus—you have both a power and a promise to take hold of. If you believe that Christ is able to save to the uttermost all who come unto God through Him (Heb. 7:25), and if you believe the hon-esty of His invitation to all who are weary and heavy-laden that they might come unto Him and find rest for their souls (Matt.

11:28–30), then you have judged Him to be faithful who has promised, and then indeed you will lay hold of Christ as the power of God unto salvation. According to the faith that has led you to fix your hope on the Saviour, so will it be done unto you. In the language of Scripture, "hold fast the confidence and the rejoicing of the hope firm unto the end" (Heb. 6:3). "Cast not away therefore your confidence, which hath great recompense of reward" (Heb. 10:35).

And if you have not yet begun to place this confidence in the assurances of the gospel, lay hold of them now. They are addressed to you. "The Spirit and the bride say, Come. And let him that heareth say, Come. And let him that is athirst come. And *whosoever will*, let him take the water of life freely" (Rev. 22:17, emphasis added). It is not a vague generality of which I am speaking. You are invited to take up with Christ, and trust in Him for yourself. God Himself urges you to repent and live (Ezek. 18:31).

I am well aware that unless the Spirit reveal to you, all I have said about Him will fall fruitless upon your ears, and your hearts will remain as cold and as heavy and as alienated as ever. Faith is His gift, and it is not of ourselves. But the minister is at his post when he puts the truth before you; and you are at your posts when you hearken diligently, and have a prayerful spirit of dependence on the Giver of all wisdom, that He will bless the Word spoken, and make it reach your souls in the form of a salutary and convincing application.

And it is indeed incredible—it is more than incredible—that we should entertain any thought that our Father who is in heaven is less than benevolent. With all the ways He sets Himself forth to us, isn't it disgraceful that we do not have more confidence in His goodness and His willingness to save? How can we account for the barrier of unbelief that stands so obstinately firm in spite of His every remonstrance? Why does the hardness continue? Not the hardness of God toward us, for He has said everything to woo us to put our trust in Him, but our hardness toward God. In the face of His kind and compassionate entreaties, how can we persist in being cold and distant and afraid of Him?

I know not, my brethren, in how far I may have succeeded, as an humble and unworthy instrument, in drawing aside the veil which darkens the face of Him who sits on the throne. But oh, how imposing is the attitude, and how altogether affecting is the argument with which He comes forward to us in the text we are considering! "Fury is not in me."

It is not so much His saying that there is no fury in Him whatsoever. He often tells us of His wrath in other passages of Scripture. But the striking peculiarity of the words now before us is the way He would convince us how little interest He can have in our destruction. He is reassuring us how far it is from His thoughts to aspire after the glory of such an achievement.

It is as if He had said, "It would be nothing to Me to consume you all by the breath of My indignation. It would throw no honor over Me to sweep away the whole strength of that rebellion which you have mustered up against Me. It would make no more to My glory than if I went through the thorns and briers and burned them before Me. This is not the battle I want to engage in—this is not the victory by which I seek to signalize Myself. And you mistake Me, you mistake Me, feeble children of men, if you think that I aspire after anything else with any one of you than that you should be prevailed on to come into My vineyard, and lay hold of My strength, and seek to make peace with Me.

"The victory that My heart is set upon is not a victory over your persons. That is a victory that will easily be gotten in the great day of final reckoning over all who have refused My overtures, and would none of My reproof, and have turned them away from my beseeching offers of reconciliation. In that great day of the power of My anger, it will be seen how easy it is to accomplish such a victory. How rapidly the fire of My conflagration will involve the rebels who have opposed Me in that devouring flame from which they never, never can be extricated! How speedily the execution of the condemning sentence will run through the multitude who stand at the left hand of the Avenging Judge! And rest assured, you who are now hearing Me, and whom I freely invite all to enter into the vineyard of God, that this is not the triumph that God is longing after."

It is not the victory over your persons in judgment that brings Him pleasure. It is the victory over your wills now. It is that you do honor to His testimony by placing your reliance on Him. It is that you accept of His kind and free assurances that He has no ill-will to you. It is that you cast the whole burden of sullen fear and suspicion away from your hearts, and that now, even now, you enter into a fellowship of peace with the God whom you have offended.

Oh, be prevailed upon! I know that terror will not subdue you. I know that all the threatenings of the Law will not reclaim you. I know that no direct process of pressing home the claims of God upon your obedience will ever compel you to the only obedience that is of any value in His estimation—even the willing obedience of the affections to a Father whom you love.

But surely when He looks on you with the countenance of a Father; when He speaks to you with the tenderness of a loving Parent; when He tries to woo you back to that house of His from which you have wandered; and when, to persuade you of His goodwill, He descends so far as to reason the matter, and to tell you that He is no more seeking any glory from your destruction than He would seek glory from lighting into a blaze the thorns and the briers, and burning them together—ah! My brethren, should it not look plain to the eye of faith how honest and sincere the God of your redemption is, who is thus bowing Himself down to the mention of such an argument?

Do lay hold of it, and be impressed by it, and cherish no longer any doubt of the goodwill of the Lord God, merciful and gracious. Let your faith work by love to Him who has done so much and said so much to call you to loving faith. And let this love manifest all the power of a commanding principle within you, by urging your every footstep to the new obedience of new creatures in Jesus Christ your Lord.

Thus, the twofold benefit of the gospel will be realized by all who believe and obey that gospel. Reconciled to God by the death of His Son, regenerated by the power of that mighty and all-subduing Spirit who is at the giving of the Son, your salvation will be complete. You will be washed, and sanctified, and justified in the name of the Lord Jesus, and by the Spirit of our God.[1]

Appendix 2

On the Love of God, and Whether It Extends to the Non-Elect

EDITOR'S NOTE: This text by Andrew Fuller, influential Baptist pastor and writer from England in the late seventeen hundreds, was excerpted from a letter to a friend.

QUESTION: Since God never intended those whom He did not elect to know the power of His grace in Christ Jesus, how can we extol the love of God in seeking the salvation of men, except in relation to those whom He designed to save?

And how can we speak of the love of God to men at large, except on the general ground that it is among the mass of mankind that His chosen can be found?

In fewer words, What is it the love God has for those whom He has not chosen to eternal life?

ANSWER: I cannot undertake to free this subject or any other from difficulty; nor do I pretend to answer it on the principles of reason. If I can ascertain certain principles to be taught in the Word of God, I feel it safe to reason from them; but if I proceed beyond this, I am at sea.

Respecting the first member of this question, I am not aware of having represented God as "seeking the salvation of those who are not saved." If by the term seeking were meant no more than His furnishing them with the means of salvation, and, as the moral Governor of His creatures, sincerely directing and inviting them to use them, I should not object to it. In this sense He said of Israel, "O that thou hadst hearkened to my commandments!" (Isa. 48:18). In this sense the Lord of the vineyard is described as seeking fruit where He finds none (Lk. 13:7). But if it be understood to include such a desire for the salvation of men as to do all that can be done to accomplish it, I do not approve of it. I see no inconsistency between God's using all proper means for the good of mankind as their Creator and Governor, and His withholding effectual grace, which is something super-added to moral government, and to which no creature has any claim,

As to the second part of the question above, God may certainly be said to exercise love to mankind, being the mass containing His chosen people. But I cannot think this idea gives a complete answer.

It appears to me an incontrovertible fact that God is represented in His Word as exercising goodness, mercy, kindness, long-suffering, and even love towards men as men. The bounties of Providence are described as flowing from *kindness* and *mercy*. Moreover, God's own kindness and mercy is held up to us as an example of how we should love our enemies (Matt. 5:44–45; Lk 6:35–36). And this the apostle extols, calling it, "the riches of his goodness," keenly censuring the wicked for despising it, instead of being led to repentance by it (Rom. 2:4).

And what if God never intended to render His goodness, forbearance, and long-suffering effectual to the leading of them to repentance? Does it follow that it is not goodness?

I read such language as this: "God so loved the world that He gave His only begotten Son, that whosoever believeth in Him should not perish, but have everlasting life." Also, the ministry of reconciliation was in this strain: "We are ambassadors for Christ, as though God did beseech [men] by us: we pray [them] in Christ's stead, be ye reconciled to God" (2 Cor. 5:20). I can draw no conclusion short of this: Eternal life through Jesus Christ is freely offered to sinners as sinners. Or as Calvin, on John 3:16, expressed it:

> He useth the universal note both that He may invite all men in general unto the participation of life, and that He may cut off all excuse from unbelievers. To the same end tendeth the term world; for although there shall nothing be found in the world that is worthy of God's favour, yet He showeth that He is favorable unto the whole world, when He calleth all men without exception to the faith of Christ. But remember that life is promised to all who shall believe in Christ, so commonly, that yet faith is not common to all men; yet God doth only open the eyes of His elect, that they may seek Him by faith.
>
> Although God sent His Son to die for the whole world and offers pardon and eternal life to all who should believe in Him, if He had done so without making effectual provision for the reception of Him by electing certain people to salvation, what would have been the consequence? Not one of the human race, you may say, would have been saved, and so Christ would have died in vain. Be it so.
>
> Though this would not have comported with the wise and gracious designs of God, yet it does not appear to me inconsistent with His justice, goodness, or sincerity. If He had called sinners to repent, believe, and be saved, while He withheld the means of salvation, it would have been so; but not in His merely withholding the grace necessary to turn the sinner's heart.

If I am not mistaken, this second member of the question proceeds on the principle that there can be no true goodwill exercised towards a sinner in inviting him to repent, believe, and be saved, unless effectual grace be given him for the purpose. But that principle appears to me unscriptural and unfounded. Supernatural, effectual, saving grace is indeed necessary to the *actual production of good* in men; but it is never represented as necessary to justify the goodness of God in *expecting or requiring it.* All that is necessary to this end is that He furnish them with rational powers, objective light, and outward means. In proof of this, let all those scriptures be considered in which God complains of men for not repenting, believing, or obeying. For example, in the complaint against Chorazin and Bethsaida, no mention is made of supernatural grace given to them: but merely of the "mighty works" wrought before them (Matt. 11:20–24).

Similarly, in the parable of the landowner, the complaint that the vinegrowers lacked reverence for the landowner's Son was not founded on his having furnished them with supernatural grace (Matt. 21:33–38). Instead, it was justified because he had provided them with objective light, means, and advantages. Likewise God gave no effectual grace to those who are accused of bringing forth wild grapes instead of grapes; yet *He looked for* and asked what He could have done more for His vineyard that He had not done (Isa. 5:4).

The strivings of the Spirit, which sinners are described as "resisting," (Acts 7:51; cf. Gen. 6:3) could not for this reason mean the effectual grace of the Holy Spirit, nor indeed any thing wrought in them, but the impressive motives presented to them by the inspired messages of the prophets (see Neh. 9:30).

That is the same way I conceive we are to understand the complaint in Deuteronomy 29:4: "The Lord hath not given you an heart to perceive, and eyes to see, and ears to hear, unto this day." It is inconceivable that Moses should complain of them for the Lord's not having given them *supernatural grace.* The complaint appears to be founded on the non-success of the most impressive *outward means*, which ought to have produced in them a heart to perceive, eyes to see, and ears to hear. Such is the scope of the passage—"Moses called unto all Israel, and said unto them, Ye have seen all that the Lord did before your eyes in the land of Egypt unto Pharaoh, and unto all his servants, and unto all his land; the great temptations which thine eyes have seen, the signs, and those great miracles: yet the Lord hath not given you an heart to perceive, and eyes to see, and ears to hear, unto this day" (Deut. 29:2–4).

From the whole, I conclude that there are two kinds of influence by which God works on the minds of men: First, *that which is common*, and which is effected by the ordinary use of motives presented to the mind for consideration. Secondly, *that which is special and supernatural*. The one is exercised by Him as the moral Governor of the world; the other as the God of grace, through Jesus Christ. The one contains nothing mysterious, any more than the influence of our words and actions on each other; the other is such a mystery that we know nothing of it but by its effects. The former *ought* to be effectual; the latter *is* so.

Finally, you sum up the question in fewer words by asking, "What is the love which God hath for those whom He hath not chosen to eternal life?" I reply, It is the goodwill of the Creator, whose tender mercies are over all His works (Ps. 145:9). It is that tender regard for the work of His hands which nothing but sin could extinguish. That is why the infliction of the most tremendous punishments is proof of sin's malignity.

Scripture implies that God's wrath is against the grain of His native goodness. Since God's tender mercies are over all His works, we know that He would not punish offenders with eternal destruction if the inalienable interests of His character and government did not require it. Such are the ideas conveyed by implication in Genesis 6:7: "I will destroy man *whom I have created* from the face of the earth" and Isaiah 27:11: "*He that made them* will not have mercy on them, and *He that formed them* will show them no favour" (emphasis added).[1]

Appendix 3

Christ the Savior of the World

EDITOR'S NOTE: This sermon by Thomas Boston, Scottish pastor and author, was preached at Ettrick, Scotland on June 7, 1724.

And we have seen and do testify that the Father sent the Son to be the Saviour of the world (1 John 4:14).

John, the beloved disciple, in his epistles, is still breathing love. Love is the string he delights peculiarly to harp upon. He is always either magnifying God's love to us, or pressing our love to God and to one another.

But his favorite subject, love, is no narrow one, but most comprehensive. It comprehends both the gospel and the law, both faith and works. The love of God to man is the great doctrine of the gospel and the object of faith. Men's love to God and to one another is the great doctrine of the law of the Ten Commandments and the object of holy practice.

There is a near relation between the two: God's love is the fountain—our love the stream. The former is the original holy fire; the latter the flame kindled by it. Accordingly, the context of

1 John 4:14 asserts how the love of God moves us to love one another. But the verse itself displays how divine love is the substance of the gospel.

Here, then, we have the gospel, which all the apostles were in one voice to preach unto the world: "We have seen and do testify that the Father sent the Son to be the Saviour of the world." And therein we may consider two things:

First, *the gospel or glad tidings itself:* that the Father sent the Son to be the Savior of the world. Here is indeed glad news to the world—Christ's mission. The promise of this mission was made to fallen Adam in paradise. Believers under the Old Testament lived and died in the faith of it. But the apostles testified it as a thing performed. Past tense: the Father sent, or has sent, the Son.

The party sent is the Son of God, our Lord Jesus Christ. No other was fit for this mission. The party sending, from whom He had His commission, was the Father—the First Person of the glorious Trinity. None of a lower dignity could send one of His dignity. The character in which He was sent, is as "Saviour of the world." The words are without any supplement; of which there is no need here. Christ was constituted, nominated, and appointed by his Father as "Saviour of the world." And thus was He sent away into the world in that character.

"The world" is the world of mankind indefinitely, ruined by Adam's sin (Jn. 3:16 ff.). Therein God's love toward mankind appeared (Tit. 3:4).

Second, we note *the certainty of this gospel or glad tidings.* All the apostles witnessed with one mouth this great truth—and they testified to it as eyewitnesses. They had seen the Savior, conversed with Him, read His commission as He unfolded it to them from the Old Testament, and beheld heaven's seal of authentication again and again in His miracles. This matter of their witnessing from their own eyesight was so crucial to the apostolic testimony that the apostle Paul, who was not called to be an apostle until after Christ's ascension, was allowed first to see with his eyes, before he should bear witness. Jesus told him, "I have appeared unto thee for this purpose, to make thee a minister and a witness both of these things which thou hast seen, and of those things in the which I will appear unto thee" (Acts 26:16).

The Doctrine

IT IS THE GREAT TRUTH AND TESTIMONY *of the gospel that the Father hath sent his Son Jesus Christ in the character of Savior of the world.*

In examining this doctrine, I shall first take notice of some things signified in the apostle John's testimony; second, unwrap the sense of the title "Savior of the world"; and third, probe the applications of this truth.

Some things signified in this testimony. First, the world needed a Savior. Otherwise one would not have been provided for them by Him who does nothing in vain. It was a sick world, cast into a desperate illness by eating of the forbidden fruit. Humanity needed a physician to cure the distemper. Jesus said, "They that be whole need not a physician, but they that are sick" (Matt. 9:12). It was a cursed world, staked down under wrath by the sentence of the broken law. Such a world needed a Savior to remove the curse and bring in the blessing. So "God, having raised up his Son Jesus, sent him to bless you" (Acts 3:26). It was a lost world—lost to God, lost to themselves, lost to all good, lost and perishing under the wrath of God. It needed Someone to seek and save: "For the Son of man is come to seek and to save that which was lost" (Luke 19:10).

Second, no one of inferior dignity to the Son of God could be the Savior of the world. No man or angel would be able to sustain the character of Savior of a lost world. The work of that office was above the reach of the whole creation (cf. Rev. 5:3). Here was a trial of the divine love to man. Humanity's case was hopeless and helpless from all the creatures. But "God so loved the world, that he gave his only begotten Son, that whosoever believeth in him should not perish, but have everlasting life" (Jn. 3:16).

Third, Christ was sent to be Savior of the world from God's own initiative. The plot to save humanity was conceived entirely without humanity's input. The world did not meet, and send someone to the court of heaven with a petition for a Savior. The Savior was not granted in response to sinners' earnest entreaties and supplications. Instead, the Father, purely out of free love, sent his Son to be the Savior of the world. The world's needs spoke loud, but they themselves were quite silent; and yet their needs spoke no louder than those of the fallen angels. Sovereign, free grace heard the voice of man's need, while it stopped its ears to the needs of fallen angels. "For verily he took not on him the nature of angels; but he took on him the seed of Abraham" (Heb. 2:16). "But after that the kindness and love of God our Savior toward *man* appeared" (Tit. 3:4, emphasis added).

Fourth, Christ is fully furnished for the saving of a lost world. His being sent in that character proves His ability to answer it. "Wherefore he is able also to save them to the uttermost that come unto God by him, seeing he ever liveth to make intercession for them" (Heb. 7:25). There is nothing wrong in the world but what there is a remedy to be found in Christ for. Whosoever in the world shall die, they shall not die because there was no help for their case in the Savior, but because they did not put their case in His hand. The Savior of the world is certainly able to save the world; since He was sent of God in that character.

Finally, the salvation of lost sinners of the world of mankind is very acceptable to the God and Father of our Lord Jesus, as well as to Jesus Himself. Otherwise God would not have sent His Son to be Savior of the world. "For this is good and acceptable in the sight of God our Saviour; who will have all men to be saved, and to come unto the knowledge of the truth" (1 Tim. 2:3–4). Hence, the salvation of sinners is called "the pleasure of the Lord," (Isa. 53:10). So He is said to make the marriage for His Son, and to send forth His servants to bid all to come to that marriage (Matt. 22:9). From this it is evident that there is no impediment on Heaven's part to the salvation of sinners by Jesus Christ. Saving sinners is pleasing to the Father, to His Son, and to His Spirit.

The sense of the title Savior of the world. In what sense is Christ Savior of the world? *Savior* is a name of honor, and a name of business. It is an honorable thing to save and help the miserable—to be destined, appointed, and called to that employment. Every such honorable post has some work annexed to it, which success is expected to attend—as in the case of a teacher, physician, and the like. In fact, teachers or physicians *are* types of "saviors" in society. They are saviors in two ways: in respect of office, and in respect of actuality. In the first sense, "savior" speaks of one called to and invested with the office of saving, teaching, or curing society. Those appointed to such an office are called teachers or physicians—saviors—even before they ever teach or cure or save anyone. In this respect one may be called an *official* savior. There is another sense in which we speak of an *actual* savior. In such cases the term is applied with respect to the actuality of saving, teaching, or healing. As the former arises from an appointment put upon such a one, this arises from the work He manages in virtue of that appointment. Thus, Nehemiah 9:27 says, "When they cried unto thee, thou heardest them from heaven; and according to thy manifold mercies thou gavest them saviours, who saved them out of the hand of their enemies."

Our Lord Jesus is the *actual* Savior of the elect only, in whose room and stead only He died upon the cross, according to the eternal covenant between Him and the Father—the covenant of grace, otherwise called the covenant of redemption (these are not two, but one and the same covenant). Thus, the apostle calls Him "the Saviour of the body," (Eph. 5:23). That is, in a particular sense He is Savior of the elect, who make up the body whereof He was appointed Head from eternity. They are the ones on whose behalf He covenanted with the Father in the eternal covenant. And He is their Savior in the sense that He actually saves them: "She shall bring forth a son, and thou shalt call his name Jesus: for he shall save his people from their sins" (Matt. 1:21). None but these will ever truly put their case in His hand or know Him as Savior. And every one of them will certainly trust Him as Savior sooner or later. "As many as were ordained to eternal life believed" (Acts 13:48). "All that the Father giveth me shall come to me" (Jn. 6:37).

Our Lord Jesus Christ is the *official* Savior, not of the elect only, but of the world of mankind indefinitely. Thus, our text calls Him "saviour of the world." In a cross reference, God in Christ is called "the saviour of all men," but in a special sense, the Savior of "those that believe," (1 Tim. 4:10).

When a governmental ruler, out of regard for his people's welfare, commissions a qualified physician to be surgeon general to all of society, the commission itself constitutes him surgeon general of that whole society. Even though many individuals should never employ him, but call other physicians, yet still there is a relation between him and them; he is their surgeon general by office.

In the same way, God, looking on the ruined world of mankind, has constituted and appointed Jesus Christ His Son Savior of the world. Christ has Heaven's patent for this office, and wherever the gospel comes, He is held up as Savior by office. By this office a relation is constituted between Him and the world of mankind. He is their Savior, and they the objects of His administration. Any of them all may come to Him as Savior, without money or price, and be saved by Him as their own Savior appointed to that office by the Father.

So the matter lies here: in this official sense, Christ is Savior of the whole world.

This appears even more clearly when we consider Scripture testimony, which is plain. Our text expressly calls Him Savior of the world. The believing Samaritans likewise profess their faith in Him: "Now we believe, not because of thy saying: for we have heard him ourselves, and know that this is indeed the Christ, the Saviour of the world" (Jn. 4:42). You have the appointment of Heaven very plainly in John 3:16: "God so loved the world, that he gave his only begotten Son, that whosoever believeth in him should not perish, but have everlasting life"—even as the brazen serpent lifted up on the pole in the wilderness was ordained by God for healing to the snake-bitten persons of the whole camp of Israel. Hence, Christ's salvation is called "the common salvation" in Jude 3; any of mankind's sinners may lay hold on this salvation. Even so the Savior's birth is said to be "good tidings of great joy, which shall be to all people" (Lk. 2:10)—which it could not have been, if He had not been a Savior to all people. And for this reason He Himself testifies that He came to save the world: "God sent not his Son into the world to condemn the world; but that the world through him might be saved" (Jn. 3:17).

In John 12:47 He states, "I came not to judge the world, but to save the world." This is His office. He is held up as Savior to all sinners generally; not to this or that sort of sinner, but to all sinners of mankind indefinitely, without exception. "This is a faithful saying, and worthy of all acceptation, that Christ Jesus came into the world to save sinners" (1 Tim. 1:15). "This is a faithful saying, and worthy of all acceptation, that Christ Jesus came into the world to save sinners." He came "to seek and to save that which was lost" (Lk. 19:10). To the same purpose He declares Himself "the light of the world" namely, by office (Jn. 8:12). And whosoever will follow Him "shall not walk in darkness, but shall have the light of life" (Jn. 8:12). That is why the gospel message He has committed to us is a message of reconciliation. We are to beseech men in Christ's stead to be reconciled to God (2 Cor. 5:19–20).

If it were not so that Christ is Savior of the world, He could not warrantably be offered with His salvation to the world indefinitely, but to the elect only. If He were not commissioned to the office of Savior of all men, it would be no more appropriate to call all men to trust Him as Savior any more than He could be offered lawfully to fallen angels (who are *not* within His commission as Savior). The gospel offer could never lawfully carry the matter beyond the bounds of Christ's commission from His Father.

But we know from Scripture that Christ and His salvation may be warrantably offered to the whole world of sinners, with assurance that whoever of them will turn in faith to Him as Savior, he shall be saved (Mark 16:15–16). Moreover, if it were not so, the unbelief of hearers of the gospel, their not coming to Christ for salvation, could not be their sin. It can never be one's sin not to do a thing he has no legitimate warrant for. No one could be held guilty for not turning to Christ for salvation, unless there is a sense in which God has appointed Him to be Savior of that guilty one. It is no sin for fallen angels not to believe in Christ for salvation, because they are not within the Savior's commission. They are not commanded to turn to Him as Savior, and even if they did so, they would find Him their judge only, and no Savior to them.

But Scripture tells us that not believing in Christ the Savior is the very sin that ruins the hearers of the gospel who ultimately perish: "And this is the condemnation, that light is come into the world, and men loved darkness rather than light, because their deeds were evil" (Jn. 3:19).

Finally, if it were not so that Christ is Savior of the world, the elect themselves could never believe in Christ until their election were revealed to them. That is contrary to the stated method of grace, for no one can believe on Christ for salvation, until that person sees Him to be a Savior for them.

There are two things further to be remarked on before we move on:

☐ First, the ground on which Christ is constituted Savior of the world is nothing but the infinite sufficiency of the merit of His death and sufferings. Christ died as a substitute for His elect in particular. The Good Shepherd lay down His life "for the sheep" (Jn. 10:15). Yet the price He paid for them was of infinite worth. It was therefore sufficient in itself to save the whole world. The bread provided for them—a crucified Christ—was sufficient to give life to and feed, not them only, but the whole world of mankind. Therefore He is appointed Savior of the world: "For the bread of God is he which cometh down from heaven, and giveth life unto the world. . . . I am the living bread which came down from heaven: if any man eat of this bread, he shall live for ever: and the bread that I will give is my flesh, which I will give for the life of the world" (Jn. 6:33, 51).

☐ Second, the title "Savior of the world" is a title of honor Christ merited by laying down His life on behalf of sinners. The Father speaks thus: "I will also give thee for a light to the Gentiles, that thou mayest be my salvation unto the end of the earth" (Isa. 49:6). The Father invested Him with "all power . . . in heaven and in earth" (Matt. 28:18). "For the Father judgeth no man, but hath committed all judgment unto the Son: That all men should honour the Son, even as they honour the Father (Jn. 5:22–23). It was a reward suitable to His work.

The business committed to Him as Savior of the world. Christ's work is to save sinners from their sin: "Thou shalt call his name Jesus: for he shall save his people from their sins" (Matt. 1:21). Satan ruined the world of men by bringing sin upon them. They were bound with the cords of guilt. The image of God in them was defaced. They were polluted and made loathsome and shut up in bondage to a strange lord.

But God has appointed Christ Savior of the world so that sinners may come to Him and be delivered from their sins. "He that committeth sin is of the devil; for the devil sinneth from the beginning. For this purpose the Son of God was manifested, that he might destroy the works of the devil" (1 John 3:8). Sin is an inveterate disease, the care of which was as far beyond the reach of any mere creature as the raising of the dead is. So He was appointed Savior in the case: "I have laid help upon one that is mighty; I have exalted one chosen out of the people" (Ps. 89:19).

Christ's work is also to save sinners from misery and to free them from destruction. "O Israel, thou hast destroyed thyself; but in me is thine help" (Hos. 13:9). People are by sin made objects of wrath, laid under the curse of the broken law, liable to revenging wrath for time and for eternity. But Christ is appointed to save them from all this, upon their coming to Him and trusting Him for that purpose. "And a man shall be as an hiding place from the wind, and a covert from the tempest; as rivers of water in a dry place, as the shadow of a great rock in a weary land" (Isa. 32:2).

Sin let in a deluge of miseries on the world. These miseries flow about the sinner continually in greater or lesser measure. But He is a Savior to deliver them from those miseries. "Of him are ye in Christ Jesus, who of God is made unto us wisdom, and righteousness, and sanctification, and redemption" (1 Cor. 1:30).

The Application

Believe. Behold here, admire, and believe the great love of God to a lost world, in providing a Savior, and such a Savior, for them—even His own Son. Scripture speaks of this in a very high strain: "God so loved the world, that he gave his only begotten Son, that whosoever believeth in him should not perish, but have everlasting life" (Jn. 3:16). There was a man-love in God: "The kindness and love of God our Saviour toward man appeared" (Tit. 3:4). That speaks of a love of the species mankind. God's love for humanity has appeared in two eminent instances: First, in securing, by an irreversible decree, the salvation of some of them; and second, in providing a Savior for the whole of the kind, constituting His own Son Savior to the lost family of Adam indefinitely.

Believe this truth with application to yourselves. If upon this a secret murmur begins to go through your heart, *But it was not for me*—crush it in the bud, for it is a bud of hell. If you are not one of the demon-kind, but one of sinful mankind, it was indeed for you. The Father gave Christ as a Savior for you, that if you would believe on Him, you should not perish. He sent His Son from heaven with full instructions and ample powers to save you, if you will believe. And is not this love? Believe it, and it will be the way to let you in to a sight of more love.

Behold here a broad and firm foundation of faith for all and every one of you. You may come to Christ whatever your case is, and you may claim His righteousness and His whole salvation for yourselves. You may hide yourselves in Him as the refuge appointed for you by the Father—a holy refuge from sin and wrath. You are as free to lay hold of Him as Savior as the bitten Israelites were to look to the brazen serpent. You may wholly trust Him to save you from sin and wrath. For He was sent by the Father as Savior of the world. And if by the Father's appointment He is Savior of the world, He is by office *your* Savior, and *my* Savior, since we are members of that world of mankind. Therefore we may by faith claim His saving us from sin and wrath.

As a child who lives in a school district may claim teaching from one who is appointed teacher of a public school; as those of a congregation may claim the preaching of their own minister; and as the wounded in battle may claim the services of a physician who has been appointed to their regiment. We "testify that the Father sent the Son to be the Saviour of the world" (1 John 4:14).

Sinners living in their sins, pining away, and about to perish eternally in sin, are without excuse. For "the Father sent the Son to be the Saviour of the world." Jesus said, "If I had not come and spoken unto them, they had not had sin: but now they have no cloak for their sin" (Jn. 15:22). Sinners are destroyed with their living and raging lusts. They are run down with them as with running sores; their souls are bleeding to death with them as with mortal wounds. In this state they hold on over the belly of their guilt and they say they cannot help it. One cannot help his swearing; another his sensuality; another his pride, passion, covetousness, gross ignorance, his old corrupt unrenewed heart. But the truth is, they do not want it helped. Jesus said, "Ye will not come to me, that ye might have life" (Jn. 5:40). If you cannot help it, you have a Savior who can help it, and would certainly help it if you would come to Him. But if you will not come, you will perish in your sin. Jesus warned, "I said therefore unto you, that ye shall die in your sins: for if ye believe not that I am he, ye shall die in your sins" (Jn. 8:24).

Know with certainty that if any of you *shall* perish—and if you go on in your sins ye shall perish—you shall not perish for want of a Savior. At the tribunal of God, the devils may say, "We could not be saved from our sins—for there was no Savior appointed for us." The pagans may say, "We could not be saved, for though we were within the compass of the Savior's commission, yet we never heard of it. It was never intimated to us." But what will *you* have to say when your Savior shall sit judge upon you and condemn you to suffer the vengeance of eternal fire? Your only reply will be that you would have none of Him or His salvation. You did not want to be saved from your sins. You would not trust Him as Savior, though He had His Father's commission to be Savior of the world—and your Savior. Though this was explained to you, you would not receive Him as your Savior. You would rather die in your sins than trust Him.

Examine yourself. Is the Savior of the world by office your actual Savior? Has He saved you? Do not think that Christ puts off His saving of sinners until they come to heaven. True, they are not *completely* saved until they see Him (1 Jn. 3:2). But if your salvation by Christ is not begun here, you shall never get there. "For it is not by works of righteousness which we have done, but according to his mercy he saved us, by the washing of regeneration, and renewing of the Holy Ghost; which he shed on us abundantly through Jesus Christ our Saviour; that being justified by his grace, we should be made heirs according to the hope of eternal life" (Tit. 3:5–7).

You have no right before the Lord to His table, if He has not been an actual Savior to you. If He has not saved you from sin and wrath initially (though not completely) you have no part with Him.

But as soon as a sinner turns to Him, He fully justifies that sinner. What are the marks of faith that follow?

First, if Christ has really begun to save you, you will have the saved man's thoughts of sin, and of the wrath of God. If a drowning man were pulled alive out of a water—or a filthy stinking puddle—and standing at the side of it, looking to it after his narrow escape, what would be his thoughts of that water, that puddle, where be was once over head and ears, and almost gone? Such will be your thoughts of sin, and of the wrath of God. You will have solemn and devout thoughts of the wrath of God above all the things you fear. "Wherefore we receiving a kingdom which cannot be moved, let us have grace, whereby we may serve God acceptably with reverence and godly fear for our God is a consuming fire" (Heb. 12:28–29). Jesus said, "Fear not them which kill the body, but are not able to kill the soul: but rather fear him which is able to destroy both soul and body in hell" (Matt 10:28). Of all terrors, divine wrath will be to you the most terrible.

Those in the state of wrath either have lost their sense of God's wrath; or they know not where they are; or they are dreaming of some pleasant place. And so they go on peacefully in their sins, undisturbed with thoughts of wrath. Or else they have some terrible apprehensions of it, but they may think there is something more terrible. Therefore they will rather sin than suffer the hardships attending the mortification of sin. Or else their heart is fire-hot with the terror of the wrath of God, and in the meantime, at least, stone-cold of love and childlike affection to the God whose wrath it is. But the saved soul looks on God's wrath as of all things the most awful, yet with a childlike reverence and affection toward that God whose wrath it is.

Second, if Christ is your Savior actually, you will have a transcendent esteem of and love to your Savior. "Unto you therefore which believe he is precious " (1 Pet. 2:7). His conscience-purifying blood, His soul-sanctifying Spirit will be more valuable to you than a thousand worlds. You will desire them above all things, pant and long after them, and seek more and more of them. In comparison of them, all the world will be but trifles in your eyes, which you would be content to part with in order to gain the riches of Christ: "[The merchant man] when he had found one pearl of great price, went and sold all that he had, and bought it" (Matt. 13:46). Jesus Himself said, "If any man come to me, and hate not his father, and mother, and wife, and children, and brethren, and sisters, yea, and his own life also, he cannot be my disciple" (Luke 14:26). But those who know Him know He is worth any price:

> "Yea doubtless, and I count all things but loss for the excellency of the knowledge of Christ Jesus my Lord: for whom I have suffered the loss of all things, and do count them but dung, that I may win Christ, and be found in him, not having mine own righteousness, which is of the law, but that which is through the faith of Christ, the righteousness which is of God by faith" (Phil. 3:8).

Third, if you have trusted Christ as your actual Savior, you will be groaning under the remains of the disease of sin you are saved from. Your conscience will bear witness that you would eagerly be wholly rid of it. "O wretched man that I am! who shall deliver me from the body of this death?" (Rom. 7:24). Your souls will be longing for the complete salvation, so that the enemies you see today you may see no more for ever. You will long for that complete victory over all your corruptions: "We ourselves groan within ourselves, waiting for the adoption, to wit, the redemption of our body" (Rom. 8:23).

Receive the Lord Jesus. Lay hold of Christ as *your* Savior, O sinners. Receive Him in that character wherein His Father sent Him—as the Savior of the world, and as your Savior. You are lost in your sins. Lost under the wrath of God. Lost under the curse of the law. So come to Him for His whole salvation. Put your case in His hand as your Savior by the Father's appointment; and slight Him no more.

Consider, first of all, that you need a Savior. Your disease of sin will ruin you, if you be not saved from it. The guilt of it will stake you down under wrath, and the wrath of God will sink you into hell. And as long as sin keeps its unbroken dominion over you, you can be sure the guilt is not removed. "They that be whole need not a physician, but they that are sick" (Matt. 9:12). "But of the tree of the knowledge of good and evil, thou shalt not eat of it: for in the day that thou eatest thereof thou shalt surely die" (Gen. 2:17).

There is no Savior besides Christ. "Neither is there salvation in any other: for there is none other name under heaven given among men, whereby we must be saved" (Acts 4:12). All others are physicians of no value. All your own endeavors will not save you—nor any thing any creature can do for you.

Moreover, He is able to save you. "He is able also to save them to the uttermost that come unto God by him, seeing he ever liveth to make intercession for them" (Heb. 7:25). Whatever be your case, there is infinite merit in His blood to take away the deepest guilt. "The blood of Jesus Christ his Son cleanseth us from all sin" (1 Jn. 1:7). There is an infinite efficacy of His Spirit to sanctify the most unholy: "And such were some of you: but ye are washed, but ye are sanctified, but ye are justified in the name of the Lord Jesus, and by the Spirit of our God" (1 Cor. 6:11). If you doubt that, you dishonor Christ and His Father who sent Him. "Then thou spakest in vision to thy holy one, and saidst, I have laid help upon one that is mighty; I have exalted one chosen out of the people" (Ps. 90:19).

He is willing to save you: "And the Spirit and the bride say, Come. And let him that heareth say, Come. And let him that is athirst come. And whosoever will, let him take the water of life freely" (Rev. 22:17). The only thing wanting is your willingness to be saved. "Woe unto thee, O Jerusalem! wilt thou not be made clean?" (Jer. 13:27). You need not fear being rejected if you come. He says, "Him that cometh to me I will in no wise cast out" (Jn. 6:37). He has taken on Him the office of Savior of the world, and He cannot refuse the business of it.

Finally, you must either receive Him as your Savior from sin and wrath, according to His commission from heaven, or you will be held guilty for refusing Him as your Savior, after His own Father—our God—has appointed and commissioned Him for that effect.

Consider how you will answer that before the judgment.

How can you receive Him and lay hold of Him? Only by faith. Only by believing on Him, by being convinced of your sin and hopeless state, and by desiring to be saved from both. Believe Christ is *your* Savior by His Father's appointment; and so wholly trust on Him as a crucified Savior, for His whole salvation, on the ground of God's faithfulness in His Word.[1]

Appendix 4

The Love of God to the World

EDITOR'S NOTE: The following text was excerpted from an essay by John Brown, one of several Scottish preachers who bore that name. He is remembered best for the work from which this text is taken.

For God so loved the world, that he gave his only begotten Son, that whosoever believeth in him should not perish, but have everlasting life (Jn. 3:16).

Let us now proceed to consider the primary source of this economy of salvation, as stated by our Lord. The love of God—the love of God to the world. "God so loved the world" (Jn. 3:16).

The advocates for the doctrine of the atonement—the doctrine that the death of the incarnate Only-begotten of God, as the victim for the sins of men, was necessary in order to the Divine mercy manifesting itself to sinners in the communication of pardon and salvation, consistently with the righteousness of his character and law; the advocates of this doctrine, have often been accused of holding that the interposition of the divine Son was necessary to produce in the bosom of His divine Father, a disposition to pity, and to save, man; and, as it has been forcibly put, "that the compassion of God rather than the souls of men, was the purchase made by the incarnate Son, when He laid down His life as a ransom." It has been said that they represent the Divinity, as a being of resentments so fierce that nothing could mitigate them but the tears and prayers, the blood and death, of His own Son.

It must be acknowledged that the doctrine of the atonement has not always been taught in "the words which become sound doctrine," and that language has sometimes been employed on the subject, by good men, which seemed to intimate rather that Christ died, in order that God might be induced to pity and save man, than that He died, because God pitied man, and was determined to save him.

The doctrine of the atonement, as taught in Scripture, however, lays no foundation for such conclusions. "God," according to its declarations, "is love," perfect in benignity, "rich in mercy." In forming conceptions on this subject, when we err, it is by defect, not by excess. Our ideas fall beneath, instead of rising above, the truth.

There was, there could be, no discordance among the persons of the Godhead, in reference to the salvation of man. The will of the Godhead is, and necessarily must be, one. We are not for a moment to suppose that the Father and the Spirit were disinclined to the salvation of man; and that the Son became incarnate, and suffered, and died, to induce Them to comply with His disposition to show favour to the guilty and ruined race. The wondrous economy of redemption is the fruit of that sovereign benignity which equally belongs to the Father, and to the Son, and to the Holy Ghost. In that economy, the Father sustains the majesty of Divinity. All is represented as originating in Him. But His holiness is the holiness of the Divinity; His justice, the justice of the Divinity; His love, the love of the Divinity.

Christ did not die that God might love man; He died because God loved man. "God commendeth His love to us in that, while we were yet sinners, Christ died for us" (Rom. 5:8).

In this was manifested the love of God toward us,
because that God sent his only begotten Son into the world,
that we might live through him. Herein is love; not that we
loved God, but that he loved us, and sent his Son to be the
propitiation for our sins (1 Jn. 4:9-10).

The atonement is thus not the cause, but the effect, of the love
of God. It is the wonderful expedient devised by infinite wisdom,
to render the manifestation of sovereign kindness to a guilty race,
not merely consistent with, but gloriously illustrative of, the righteousness of the Divine character, as displayed both in the
requisitions and sanctions of that holy law which man had violated.

That law is not an arbitrary institution. It is simply the embod-
iment of those principles which are necessary to the happiness of
intelligent, responsible beings, while they continue what they are,
and God continues what He is. That law originates not in sovereignty, but in that union of perfect wisdom, holiness, and
benignity, which forms the moral character of God; and to uphold
that law is a necessity of His nature; He cannot but require truth,
righteousness, and benignity of man. This law had been violated
by man. The consequence was, man became liable to the dreadful consequences of transgression. He had sinned, and he
deserved to die. The hopeless, the everlasting, destruction of the
sinner, must have seemed to every created mind the necessary
result of this state of things. But "God who is rich in mercy," and
infinite in wisdom, devised and executed a plan by which the
honor of the law might be vindicated, and yet the violators of that
law pardoned and saved; by which the evil of sin might be exhib-
ited to the intelligent universe in a light far stronger than if the
whole race of man bad perished for ever, and yet an innumerable
multitude of that self-ruined race be rescued from destruction,
and "saved . . . with an everlasting salvation" (Isa. 45:17).

The only begotten Son, in glad compliance with the merciful
appointment of His Father, having taken the place of the guilty;

and in their nature, and in their room, yielded a perfect obedience, in circumstances of the greatest temptation and difficulty, to that law which they had violated, thus showing the reasonableness and excellence of all its requisitions; and submitted in their room to such sufferings as, in the estimation of infinite wisdom and righteousness, more signally honored the sanctionary part of the Divine law, than the everlasting punishment of sinful men could have done:—"God hath set forth his Son to be a propitiation through faith in his blood, to declare his righteousness for the remission of sins, that he might be just, and the justifier of him that believes in Jesus" (Rom. 3:25-26); "a just God, and a Saviour" (Isa. 14:21).

Having thus endeavored to show that the atonement of Christ is not the procuring cause of God's love to sinners, but the means which God in his wisdom devised for rendering the display of his love consistent with his righteousness, I go on to illustrate, somewhat more particularly, the great truth upon which, in this part of the subject, I wish to fix your attention: that the whole of that wondrous economy of salvation unfolded by our Lord, proceeds from the love of God, from the love of God to the world.

The Love of God, the Origin of the Plan of Salvation

WE MAY BEGIN WITH asking in what could the plan of salvation originate but in love—pure, sovereign benignity? Contemplate the attributes and relations of God, and then contemplate the character and circumstances of man. Look first at the bestower, and then look at the recipients of salvation, and say, from what source it could flow but from spontaneous kindness?

Look upwards to Divinity and say if anything but sovereign kindness could have actuated Him in devising and executing the plan of human salvation? It could not be strict justice that influenced him: that would have led to the infliction of punishment, not the conferring of benefits; that would have led to man's destruction, not his salvation. Selfish considerations are, from the absolute independence of the Divine Being, entirely out of the question. The sources of the Divine happiness, like the sources of the Divine excellence, are in the Divine nature. No creature can either advance or diminish the happiness of God. Our gratitude, obedience, and praise for the benefits of salvation, cannot increase His felicity. Our goodness extendeth not to him (Ps. 16:2). "Can a man be profitable to God, as he that is wise is profitable to himself? Is it any pleasure to the Almighty, that thou art righteous? or is it gain to him, that thou makest thy ways perfect?" (Job 22:2-3). And if this wondrous plan of salvation could not originate in a selfish desire for our services and praises, it could as little originate in a selfish fear of our enmity, reproaches, or rebellious attempts against His government. The very idea is as absurd as it is blasphemous. "Will he reprove thee for fear of thee?" (Job 22:4). "If thou sinnest, what doest thou against him? or if thy transgressions be multiplied, what doest thou unto him?" (Job 35:6). "Thy wickedness may hurt a man as thou art" (v. 8)—but not God. He can easily render all the attempts which men and devils can make against His government, but so many occasions for the display of his wisdom, his power, and his righteousness. Had the whole sinning race of man been consigned to endless perdition, would He not have gathered through eternity a revenue of praise from their sufferings, as illustrations of His immaculate holiness, His inflexible justice, His inviolable faithfulness, without any disparagement of His benignity, which would indeed have been manifested in their interminable sufferings, as in those of the "angels who kept not their first estate" (Jude 6) such inflections being direct means of upholding that law, which is as necessary to the happiness of His intelligent creatures, as it is to the honor of His character, or the stability of His throne?

When we thus look upward to God, the giver of the blessings of the Christian salvation, we are constrained to say, "Nothing but love could influence Him in bestowing them." And when we direct our thoughts to the recipients of these benefits, we are conducted by a very short process of reasoning to the same conclusion. There is nothing in the situation or character of man which can lead us to trace blessings conferred on him to anything but pure benignity.

Man is a creature, and therefore, strictly speaking, he can have no claim on God. It was of God's free sovereign pleasure to create him, or not to create him; and when He created him, it was of His sovereign pleasure that He made him a living, thinking, immortal being, rather than an irrational brute, or an inanimate clod. As a creature, man, in common with all creatures, must be a pensioner on Divine bounty for every blessing. But though in no case could man have had a claim on God, had he continued what God made him, an innocent, a holy being, we may safely affirm that the equity as well as the benignity of God, would have secured for him everything necessary to true and permanent happiness.

But man is a sinner. He is guilty of innumerable violations of that holy law, one transgression of which deserves everlasting destruction; and he is not, as the economy of grace finds him, a penitent sinner. No, he is a hardened rebel, "going on in his trespasses," receding farther and farther from God. When God looks down from heaven on the children of men, what does He see? They have all gone aside; they have altogether become filthy; there is none that doeth good, no, not one (Ps. 14:2-3)

What could induce God to spare, what could induce Him to save, such beings? Holiness, justice, wisdom, had they not in the Divine nature been conjoined with infinite benignity, would have suggested anything rather than "thoughts of good" towards such a polluted, rebellious, worse than useless, mischievous, class of creatures; a set of beings whom a mere act of will could have annihilated, or punished with "everlasting destruction." What but love, pure sovereign compassion, could have said, "Deliver these from going down to the pit; I have found a ransom" (Job 33:24).

As it is thus plain that nothing but love could have been the source of the economy of human salvation, so it is equally evident, that that love must have had "a height and a depth, a length and a breadth" that exceeds the computing powers of created intelligences (Eph. 3:17-19). Well may we with the apostle stand in adoring wonder and exclaim, "Behold what manner of love!" (1 Jn. 3:1). "Herein"—herein indeed—"is love" (1 Jn. 4:10), as if all the other displays of Divine benignity were unworthy of regard when compared with this.

There are two ways by which we naturally measure the strength of a benevolent affection: the intrinsic value of the benefits bestowed on the objects of it; and the expense, labour, and suffering at which these benefits are obtained for them. Let us apply, or rather attempt to apply, these measures to the case before us, and we shall be obliged to confess, that this love it passes knowledge (Eph. 3:19).

The salvation which is by Christ includes deliverance from numerous, varied, immense, unending evils. It is deliverance from "perishing." It includes also restoration to numerous, varied, immense, unending blessings. It is the enjoyment of "eternal life." It is deliverance from evil, moral and physical, in all its forms, and in all its degrees, for ever and ever; and the possession of a happiness suited to, and filling to an overflow, all our capacities of enjoyment during the whole eternity of our being. When we think of the number, and variety, and value of the heavenly and spiritual blessings bestowed on us, we must acknowledge that it is "great love" wherewith God loves us; when we reflect on the inheritance, incorruptible, undefiled, and that fadeth not away, we are constrained to say, the mercy which bequeaths it, "is abundant mercy." This measure we can but very inadequately apply. Only the hopelessly lost know what the salvation of Christ delivers from. Only the blessed in heaven know what the salvation of Christ exalts to.

The God Who Loves

Even they know these things imperfectly. Eternity will be ever disclosing new horrors in the one, new glories in the other.

If we attempt to apply the second principle, we soon arrive at the same result. To obtain these blessings, the Son of God must become incarnate, and obey, and suffer, and die. God spared not his own Son, but delivered him up in our room as the victim for our transgressions (Rom. 8:32). He made Him who knew no sin, a sin offering in our room (2 Cor. 5:21). He made to meet on Him the iniquities of us all. It pleased the Lord to bruise Him; and He was wounded for our iniquities, bruised for our transgressions, and the chastisement of our peace was on Him (Isa. 53:5-6). He who was in the form of God, and who thought it not robbery to be equal with God, made himself of no reputation, took on him the form of a servant, humbled himself, and became obedient to death, even the death of the cross (Phil. 2:6-8). If it was a strong proof of the regard of Abraham to God, that he did not withhold his son, his only son, from Him, how shall we estimate the love of God to a lost world, which led Him to give His own, His only begotten, His beloved Son, that He might give Himself, a sacrifice and an offering for man's salvation!

Love of God to the World: The Origin of the Plan of Salvation

THERE IS ANOTHER IDEA to which I wish for a little to turn your attention on this part of the subject. The love in which the economy of salvation originates, is love to the world. God so loved the world as to give His only begotten Son. The term "world" is here just equivalent to mankind. It seems to be used by our Lord with a reference to the very limited and exclusive views of the Jews. They thought God loved them, and hated all the other nations of mankind. These were their own feelings, and they foolishly thought that God was altogether such an one as themselves. They

222

accordingly expected that the Messiah was to come to deliver Israel, and to punish and destroy the other nations of the earth. But God's ways were not their ways, nor His thoughts their thoughts. As the heavens are high above the earth, so were His ways above their ways, and His thoughts above their thoughts (Isa. 55:8-9).

Some have supposed that the word "world" here is descriptive not of mankind generally, but of the whole of a particular class, that portion of mankind who, according to the Divine purpose of mercy, shall ultimately become partakers of the salvation of Christ. But this is to give to the term a meaning altogether unwarranted by the usage of Scripture. There can be no doubt in the mind of a person who understands the doctrine of personal election, that those who are actually saved are the objects of a special love on the part of God; and that the oblation of the Savior had a special design in reference to them. But there can be as little doubt, that the atonement of Christ has a general reference to mankind at large; and that it was intended as a display of love on the part of God to our guilty race. Not merely was the atonement offered by Christ Jesus sufficient for the salvation of the whole world, but it was intended and fitted to remove out of the way of the salvation of sinners generally every bar which the perfections of the Divine moral character and the principles of the Divine moral government presented. Without that atonement, no sinner could have been pardoned in consistency with justice. In consequence of that atonement, every sinner may be, and if he believe in Jesus certainly shall be, pardoned and saved. Through the medium of this atonement, the Divine Being is revealed to sinners, indiscriminately, as gracious and ready to forgive; and the invitations and promises warranting men to confide in Christ for salvation, are addressed to all, and are true and applicable to all without exception or restriction.

The revelation of mercy made in the gospel refers to men as sinners, not as elect sinners. Their election or their non-election is something of which, when called on to believe the gospel, they are necessarily entirely ignorant, and with which they have nothing to do. "The kindness and love of God . . . toward man," the Divine philanthropy, is revealed (Tit. 3:4). "God was in Christ, reconciling the world unto himself" (2 Cor. 5:19). He appears in the revelation of mercy as the God who has no pleasure in the death of the wicked; who willeth all men to be saved and to come to the knowledge of the truth (Ezek. 33:11; 1 Tim. 2:3-4). "The grace of God" revealed in the gospel "brings salvation to all," without exception, who in the faith of the truth will receive it (Tit. 2:11).

I am persuaded that the doctrine of personal election is very plainly taught in Scripture; but I am equally persuaded that the minister misunderstands that doctrine who finds it, in the least degree, hampering him in presenting a full and a free salvation as the gift of God to every one who hears the gospel; and that the man abuses the doctrine who finds in it anything which operates as a barrier in the way of his receiving, as a sinner, all the blessings of the Christian salvation, in the belief of the truth. Indeed, when rightly understood, it can have no such effect. For what is that doctrine, but just this, in other words—It is absolutely certain that a vast multitude of the race of man shall be saved through Christ? And it is as certain, that if any one of those to whom that salvation is offered, remains destitute of it, and perishes eternally, it is entirely owing to his own obstinate refusal of what is freely, honestly, presented to him. The kindness of God, as manifested in the gift of His Son, is kindness to the race of man; and when, as an individual, I credit the kindness of God to man, so strangely displayed, so abundantly proved, I cannot find any reason why I should not depend on this kindness, and expect to be saved even as others.

Whenever a man hesitates about placing his dependence on the mercy of God, because he is not sure whether he be elected or not, he gives clear evidence that he does not yet understand the gospel. He does not apprehend the manifestation of the love of God to man. When he sees God in Christ reconciling the world to Himself, he does not need to ask, *Is the plan of mercy such as I am warranted to embrace? may I not somehow be excluded from availing myself of it?* These, and similar suggestions, which draw away his mind from the voice of God to the speculations of his own mind, are no more regarded." He sees God rich in mercy, ready to forgive; just, and the justifier of the ungodly. He cannot but place his confidence in Him. "Jehovah," as it has been happily said, "by the manifestation of what he has done, especially in sending Christ, and delivering Him up, the just in the room of the unjust, pleads His own cause with such subduing pathos that there is no more power of resistance: but the person who is the object of the demonstration yields himself up to the authority and glory of the truth. The sinner, thus cordially believing the Gospel, gladly and gratefully receives "the Savior of the world" as his Savior, and trusts that by the grace of God he shall partake of "the common salvation."

Notes

Chapter 1 ※ *God So Loved the World*

1. Cited in Iain H. Murray, Jonathan Edwards: *A New Biography* (Edinburgh: Banner of Truth, 1987), 169.

2. Charles G. Finney, *Revivals of Religion* (Old Tappan, New Jersey: Revell, n. d.), 4-5.

3. Ibid., 220-21 (emphasis added).

4. J. C. Pollock, Moody: *A Biographical Portrait of the Pacesetter in Modern Evangelism* (New York: Macmillan, 1963), 72-73.

5. D. L. Moody himself was undoubtedly guilty of an overemphasis on divine love. "His [one] message, aside from the constant stress on the need for conversion, was of the love of God. His theology, although basically orthodox, was ambiguous to the point of seeming not to be theology at all." George M. Marsden, *Fundamentalism and American Culture* (Oxford: Oxford, 1980), 32, cf. 35.

As a result, Moody failed to reckon with the dangers of liberalism. "While he disapproved of liberalism in the abstract, he cultivated friendships with influential liberals in the hope that peace would prevail." Ibid., 33.

The schools Moody founded in Northfield, Massachusetts, and

with which he was associated until his death, were totally dominated by liberal leadership within a generation of Moody's passing. The Moody Bible Institute in Chicago, which Moody entrusted to sound leadership several years before his death, remains strongly evangelical to this day.

6. This method of biblical criticism is still followed today by such groups as the highly publicized "Jesus Seminar," whose scholars have concluded that only thirty-one of the more than seven hundred sayings attributed to Jesus were really spoken by Him.

7. Harry Emerson Fosdick, *Christianity and Progress* (New York: Revell, 1922), 173-74 (emphasis added).

8. Ibid., 174.

9. Ibid (emphasis added).

10. That is precisely the language used by Harold Kushner, *When Bad Things Happen to Good People* (New York: Shocken, 1981).

11. Arthur W. Pink, *The Sovereignty of God* (Grand Rapids: Baker, 1930), 29-31, 245-52, 311-14.

12. Ibid., 29-30.

13. Ibid., 246.

14. Ibid., 314. The sections I quote here were removed in the edition of Pink's work published by *The Banner of Truth Trust* (1961). In his biography of Arthur Pink, editor Iain Murray called Pink's denial of God's love for the non-elect an "area of serious weakness." Iain Murray, *The Life of Arthur W. Pink* (Edinburgh: Banner of Truth, 1981), 196.

15. This is not to suggest that God is ambivalent. God is perfectly consistent with Himself (2 Tim. 2:13). Contradictory volitions cannot exist in His mind. What I am saying is this: God in a real and sincere sense hates the wicked because of their sin; yet in a real and sincere sense He also has compassion, pity, patience, and true affection for them because of His own loving nature.

16. John Calvin, *Commentary on a Harmony of the Evangelists, Matthew, Mark, and Luke*, William Pringle, trans. (Grand Rapids: Baker, 1979 reprint), 123.

17. Ibid., 125 (italics in original).

18. See appendix 3 for specific quotations from these authors.

Chapter 2 ⬛ God Is Love

1. Mary Baker Eddy, *Science and Health with Key to the Scriptures* (Boston: Trustees of MBE, 1875), 473.

2. The Children of God sect, otherwise known as the Family of Love, have been known to practice an evangelistic technique they call "love bombing," where cult members offer potential recruits sex "to show them the love of God." [Maurice C. Burrell, *The Challenge of the Cults* (Grand Rapids: Baker, 1981), 44–45.]

3. Gordon H. Clark, *First John: A Commentary* (Jefferson, Maryland: Trinity Foundation, 1980), 131.

4. John R. W. Stott, *The Epistles of John* (Grand Rapids: Eerdmans, 1964), 160.

5. Ibid.

6. Donald W. Burdick, *The Letters of John the Apostle* (Chicago: Moody, 1985), 351.

7. D. Martyn Lloyd-Jones, *The Love of God* (Wheaton: Crossway, 1994), 45.

8. Ibid., 150-53.

9. Ibid., 153-54.

10. Ibid., 51.

11. Ibid., 52 (emphasis added).

Chapter 3 ⬛ Behold the Goodness . . .

1. A. W. Tozer, *The Knowledge of the Holy* (New York: Harper & Row, 1961), 9.

2. *Westminster Confession of Faith,* chap. 2 sec. 1.

3. See Alexander Hislop, *The Two Babylons* (Neptune, New Jersey: Loizeaux, reprint of 1916 edition) for abundant historical evidence that the Babylonian religion founded by Nimrod is the basis for virtually all subsequent false religious systems.

4. W. Graham Scroggie, *The Unfolding Drama of Redemption,* 3 vols. (Grand Rapids: Zondervan, 1970) 1:383.

5. Hugh Martin, *The Prophet Jonah: His Character and Mission to Nineveh* (Grand Rapids: Baker, 1979 reprint).

Chapter 4 ▪ . . .And the Severity of God

1. Louis Berkhof, *Systematic Theology* (Grand Rapids: Eerdmans, 1941), 513.

2. Charles Lee Feinberg, *The Minor Prophets* (Chicago: Moody, 1977), 197.

Chapter 5 ▪ Everything I Need to Know About the Love of God I Learned in the Nursery?

1. John Calvin, *Commentary on a Harmony of the Evangelists, Matthew, Mark, and Luke,* William Pringle, trans. (Grand Rapids: Baker, 1979 reprint), 123.

Chapter 6 ▪ The Love of God for Humanity

1. Arthur W. Pink, *The Sovereignty of God* (Grand Rapids: Baker, 1930), 314.

2. This is the formulation of the Westminster Confession of Faith with regard to the sufficiency of Scripture: "The whole counsel of God, concerning all things necessary for his own glory,

man's salvation, faith, and life, is either expressly set down in scripture, or by good and necessary consequence may be deduced from scripture: unto which nothing at any time is to be added, whether by new revelations of the Spirit, or traditions of men" (1:6, emphasis added).

3. John Brown, *Discourses and Sayings of Our Lord*, 3 vols. (Edinburgh: Banner of Truth, 1990 reprint), 1:34.

4. B. B. Warfield, *The Saviour of the World* (Edinburgh: Banner of Truth, 1991 reprint), 114.

5. Ibid., 120-21.

6. R. L. Dabney, *Discussions: Evangelical and Theological*, 3 vols. (Edinburgh: Banner of Truth, 1982 reprint), 1:312.

7. John Calvin, *Commentary on a Harmony of the Evangelists*, Matthew, Mark, and Luke, William Pringle, trans. (Grand Rapids: Baker, 1979 reprint), 123.

8. Erroll Hulse, "The Love of God for All Mankind," *Reformation Today* (Nov-Dec 1983), 18-19.

9. Ibid., 21-22.

10. Ibid., 18.

Chapter 7 ※ The Love of God for His Elect

No *Notes*.

Chapter 8 ※ Finding Security In the Love of God

1. B. B. Warfield, *Selected Shorter Writings* (Phillipsburg, New Jersey: Presbyterian & Reformed,), 393.

2. *The Westminster Confession of Faith*, a strongly Calvinistic document, underscores this very point: "God from all eternity did, by the most wise and holy counsel of his own will, freely and

unchangeably ordain whatsoever comes to pass: yet so, as thereby neither is God the author of sin, nor is violence offered to the will of the creatures, nor is the liberty or contingency of second causes taken away, but rather established" (3.1).

Appendix 1: Fury Not in God

1. Thomas Chalmers was a Glasgow pastor and professor of theology at the University of Edinburgh in the first half of the 1800s. He led the formation of the Free Church of Scotland in 1843, after seceding from the Church of Scotland because of encroaching unbelief in the state church. He is remembered as one of the finest preachers Scotland has ever produced. His evangelistic fervor, for which he is well remembered, is evident in this tract adapted from one of his best-known sermons. It has been edited slightly, chiefly to update some of the archaic expressions.

Appendix 2: On the Love of God, and Whether It Extends to the Non-Elect

1. This is excerpted from a letter to a friend, by Andrew Fuller (1754-1815). Fuller was an influential English Baptist pastor and writer. A Calvinist who strongly opposed hyper-Calvinism, Fuller helped found the Baptist Foreign Missionary Society, which sent William Carey to India.

Appendix 3: Christ the Savior of the World

1. A sermon by Thomas Boston, preached immediately before the celebration of the Lord's Supper, at Ettrick, Scotland, on June 7, 1724. Boston was a Scottish pastor and author, best

known today for his book *Human Nature in Its Fourfold State* (Edinburgh: Banner of Truth).

Appendix 4: The Love of God to the World

1. John Brown (1784-1858) was one of several Scottish preachers who bore that name. He was known for his biblical exposition and is remembered best for the work from which this essay is excerpted—Discourses and Sayings of Our Lord Jesus Christ, 3 Vols. (Edinburgh: Banner of Truth, 1990 reprint), 1:28-36.

Scripture Index

Scripture Index

Subject Index

The God Who Loves

Subject Index

Subject Index

ABOUT THE AUTHOR . . .

DR. JOHN MACARTHUR, JR. is the dynamic pastor/teacher of Grace Community Church in Sun Valley, California. His unwavering advocacy for a restoration of biblical theology in our time has won him the respect of both serious students of the Word and "people in the pew." His numerous books include *The Vanishing Conscience, Rediscovering Expository Preaching, Ashamed of the Gospel*, and *Our Sufficiency in Christ*. Dr. MacArthur is heard daily on the nationally syndicated radio broadcast, "Grace to You," which has sold more than ten million tapes.

CPSIA information can be obtained at www.ICGtesting.com
Printed in the USA
LVOW040156120512

281352LV00005B/2/P